Turning Bowls

Dick Sing

Text written with and
photography by Donna S. Baker

4880 Lower Valley Road, Atglen, PA 19310 USA

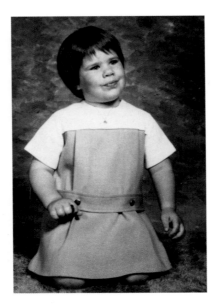

Dedication

To my daughter, Connie (Sing) Powers. One of my biggest fans, starting from childhood, and continuing as a mature woman. Who boasts about her daddy, has given me two grandsons, a sense of pride, and many years of encouragement, not to mention a few gray hairs.

Contents

Copyright © 2003 by Dick Sing
Library of Congress Control Number: 2002117296

Designed by Joseph M. Riggio Jr.
Gallery set-up by Cindy Sing

Type set in Zapf Calligraphy/Souvenir Lt BT

ISBN: 0-7643-1795-4
Printed in China

Published by Schiffer Publishing Ltd.
4880 Lower Valley Road
Atglen, PA 19310
Phone: (610) 593-1777; Fax: (610) 593-2002
E-mail: Info@schifferbooks.com
Please visit our web site catalog at
www.schifferbooks.com
We are always looking for people to write books on new and related subjects. If you have an idea for a book, please contact us at the above address.

This book may be purchased from the publisher.
Include $3.95 for shipping.
Please try your bookstore first.
You may write for a free catalog.

In Europe, Schiffer books are distributed by
Bushwood Books
6 Marksbury Avenue
Kew Gardens
Surrey TW9 4JF England
Phone: 44 (0) 20 8392 8585
Fax: 44 (0) 20 8392 9876
E-mail: Bushwd@aol.com
Free postage in the UK. Europe: air mail at cost.

Introduction

A Bowl is Like a Child

Each one is like an individual offspring yet each one has a different personality and problems. Some sleep all night with little difficulty while others raise havoc. At the "teenage" level, we encounter indecision (what should they/it look like), acne, blemishes, cracks, knots, wormholes…DAD!!! "Midlife crisis" is like torn grain, indecisive shape, and lack of direction. The final culmination is an aura, which includes good looks and shape that inspires that feeling of accomplishment. Hopefully our end product, with its even walls, good shape, and a clean surface will stimulate one's senses to recognize its uniqueness other than just the beauty of the wood's grain. Shape, balance and one's creativity rule!!! Makes one proud.

Gentleman Turner

I am not a production bowl turner, nor could I be one. Though I love to turn bowls, I could not spend my entire day turning them unless that was my only source of income. Being retired, I have the luxury of having a retirement check at the end of the month and am covered by insurance. This is something most self-employed turners do not have. I am blessed, as I do not have a quota to meet or anyone to answer to other than my best friend (Cindy, my wife). At this stage in my life, that's everything.

Why another bowl book? Because of all the turners I have encountered who have expressed the desire for me to write a book on bowls, and the friends and family who have posed questions and encouraged me in this endeavor. I have enjoyed turning one-of-a-kind bowls and the experience of working with all of the different types and species of woods that have taught me some of their quirks. I hope I can pass on some of my experiences, problems, and my love of the lathe while keeping your interest as you read.

Keeping it Fun

There are turners unwilling to admit they have problems because they feel embarrassed or have no one to turn to for help. The best solution to a problem is to be open, admit to having a problem, and seek help in solving it.

Turning a quality bowl is not as easy as it seems; indeed, some turners may never turn a perfect bowl. But who cares as long as a person gives his or her best endeavor? They may create beautiful music, lay perfect masonry, complete crossword puzzles without a dictionary, or have another gift at which they excel. Each person has his or her own special forte. The most important thing is to enjoy what you do and have fun doing it. A lathe should be fun. Why would anyone buy a lathe as punishment? Turning on a lathe should bring gratification, build one's ego and personal pride, give a feeling of accomplishment, make use of one's personal expression, and possibly add to personal gain. It's like having Christmas in July. It can become an addiction because you keep wanting to improve your skills and test your imagination. It can lead to an exclusion of your other equipment, such as table saws, thickness planer, jointer, and disc sander—unless you are into segmented turning (polychromatic).

I am not fond of the word "faster" when referring to tools or methods. Very few turners make their entire income from turning. Production turners need to be aware of techniques and methods that will make their job faster and they will find them if they are to be successful. To them, time is money. For the average turner, however, the time spent on the lathe is time for personal "R & R." Speed in completing a project should not enter into the picture, as each person has his or her own pace of doing things. Some people feel inferior in relation to other turners who accomplish things more quickly than they do. Frustration in the beginning is natural and will eventually give way to relaxation and satisfaction as you gain experience and knowledge. Practice never hurts; it will advance your learning curve. Speed comes with knowledge, practice, confidence, and desire.

Every turner's dream is to produce the perfect bowl. I like a simple bowl, a plain Jane with the ultimate curves. The simple bowl, pleasingly contoured, is one of the most difficult shapes to achieve. This is my personal preference. To me, the feel of a well-turned bowl is something that is hard to express. It may look good, but upon picking it up, if it is bottom heavy or does not feel comfortable when being held, it has lost its merit as a quality bowl. The bowl should jump into your hand and say hold me, feel me, touch me. If it doesn't, it is just another pretty piece of wood.

Bowls range from those that are utilitarian and may be used to hold change, salads, or fruit to those whose sole purpose is to be esthetically pleasing. A wildly figured burl bowl with buttered popcorn stains may be abhorrent to some turners, but once you have given that bowl to someone else, it is now their child, to do with as they like.

You may find the qualities that give a bowl its character are the same ones that make turning it difficult. Outstanding figure, burl, curl pattern—each presents its own problems and each has its own solution. In this book, I have shown a variety of woods and shapes, each with its own difficulties (which may change from one blank to the next, even if cut out of the same piece of wood). Bowl turning is ever changing—what works well today may not be handled the same way tomorrow.

As we go through our bowls, conditions and situations change. I wish I could use one bowl to show all of the situations you may encounter, but each bowl is unique in itself. You may have to refer to the various bowls in this book for specific techniques where applicable. My intent is not to confuse you by referring to other areas, but to help you understand that not everything can be explained at a given time. Throughout the book I may repeat myself many times through necessity, and because I feel the subject is important enough to be brought up again. Each situation has its own circumstances and I reserve my right to use poetic license. This book is intended to provide you with guidelines and help you with problem solving. Keep in mind that my way is not the only way. There are always alternative ways to accomplish a specific problem. If everyone approached this the same way, we would not need all the books and assorted tools. Being human and having experienced these situations, I will try to pave the road and make it less rocky. Bear with me and, as in my previous books, one thing I ask is please read the book. The pictures are nice and hopefully do tell a story, but there are a thousand words between them that create the whole picture.

Safety First

Most, not all, accidents can be avoided by being aware and vigilant of your surroundings. The "most" part is because there is always someone who throws a monkey wrench into the situation—which changes everything. You must therefore also be aware of people around you. For safety, you want to always make sure you keep your equipment in top shape. In addition, be aware of any cracks in the wood, bark inclusions and foreign objects, including live grubs. (From personal experience, let me tell you that they sure can mess up a face shield and are not the most tasty.) Gloves, long sleeves, sloppy loose clothing, cloth rags, and uncontained long hair have no place around rotating machinery. These can easily be caught up in moving parts, causing a serious injury. A face shield or safety glasses should be worn at all times. This should not be taken lightly—accidents happen in the blink of an eye, not giving you time to react. A large chunk of wood thrown from a lathe can do you, anyone around you, or your shop devastating damage. Awareness is a way of life around machinery.

Dust is also another problem not to be overlooked. Spalted woods, some exotics, and even some of our domestic woods can become real health hazards. Not every turner is affected in the same way by the same woods. Just be aware of these. Dust masks, a good dust collection system, or even a fan in a window can make breathing easier and safer.

Another hazard is that a lathe produces a lot of sanding dust. If it is allowed to gather, it can become a very volatile explosive. The finer the dust, the greater the danger. Cleaning your shop on a regular basis will not only help this situation, but will keep your floor clean in general, which is also less hazardous.

Attune yourself to what is happening as you turn—sight, sound, touch, heat sensation, smell, and so on all come into play. Apply all your senses when working with tools, just as one listens to and observes the different parts of a symphony. Pay attention to the hum of the motor, the sound of the belt, the cutting sound of the tools, the tic tic tic of a tool coming into contact with a crack or foreign object, heat, vibrations, the condition of the shavings, etc. Recognize safe speed and practice it at all times.

Tools, Chucks, and Equipment

Tools

In this section, I am going to review the tools that I normally use in turning a bowl. Number one, there is no "magic tool." Sure, some tools will work better than others in a given situation, but it always boils down to having your tools sharp and understanding the function of each one. Until you understand each tool's function and learn the feel and sound of how the tool is working, you will forever be looking for that "magic tool."

I also believe that most turners worry too much about specific angles on their tools. A decent turner can adjust the tool's position as needed to make it cut proficiently. There are times when steeper or shallower angles are necessary to get into a given area; for example, a shallow spindle gouge will not ride the bevel at the bottom of a deep bowl. A bowl gouge with a steep angle will not foul out on the rim and will still ride the bevel across the bottom of a bowl.

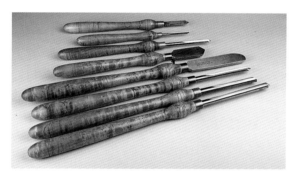

An overall look at the tools used for turning bowls. I will describe those used most often as we continue. Top to bottom: (1) 1/8" parting tool; (2) 1/4" spindle gouge; (3) 3/8" spindle gouge; (4) heavy dual angle shear scraper; (5) heavy radiused scraper; (6) 9/16" spindle gouge; (7) 5/8" acute grind bowl gouge; (8) 5/8" 30 degree bowl gouge.

This is a 5/8" diameter **bowl gouge**. It has been ground with a steep nose bevel, which will place the tool at an acute angle to the cutting surface. In other words, it will get to the bottom of a bowl but can still be used on the outside of a bowl to remove a lot of material quickly. On this gouge, the wings have been ground or pulled back to provide for shear cutting. This grind normally does not come standard from the manufacturer. I do grind my tools free hand, which seems to be very challenging for a lot of less experienced turners. If you have difficulty learning to grind free hand, there are jigs available that will help you. The main thing is that you have a facet free cutting edge and are able to attain repeatability of the edge. Although I do have a jig, I rarely use it as it takes too long to set it up for my taste. If I didn't have the ability to grind free hand, however, I would definitely be using a grinding jig.

This view shows the bevel rubbing on the outside of the bowl. This would be a very good position to use when removing a lot of material, such as during the roughing out process.

This tool can also function in the shear mode, used when finishing the surface. A properly shear cut surface requires very little sanding—another good reason to learn this technique. As seen, the tool is placed at approximately a 45 degree angle to the surface being cut. The bevel is not rubbing, it is—for lack of a better word—being dragged along the surface in a controlled manner. This requires smooth body movements, as the tool will cut the surface in accord with your body movements. If your movements are ragged or jerky, your surface will reflect this. In contrast, if your movements are smooth and flowing, the surface will reflect this as well. As long as we're talking about body movements, note that they do not pertain strictly to this tool, but rather to every tool in the turner's repertoire. These are only two ways to explain the basic functions, but as you develop your skills you will find many ways to use this tool to even greater advantage.

This is another 5/8" bowl gouge, ground differently. This one is ground to approximately 30 degrees. It is much more like a spindle gouge than a bowl gouge. I like it because its shallower angle gives it the ability to cleanly cut shallow bowls and platters. At times, it will even cut problem grain better than the acute gouge. Of course, the reverse can also be true.

When riding the bevel, the 30 degree bowl gouge cuts a very clean shaving.

Here the 30 degree grind is at a much shallower angle than on the other gouge. Down close to the chuck, I would not be able to ride the bevel on the 30 degree grind because the tool would interfere with the chuck and foul out, lifting the bevel off of the cutting surface. The other gouge, with its acute tip, would be a much better choice in that area.

Here the 30 degree grind tool is used in a shearing cut. The cut achieved with this bowl gouge is basically the same as with the other one. Why bother having two of the same bowl gouges ground differently, then? Number one, I am a tool junkie. Number two, there are certain problem situations where one tool will outshine the other. I happen to be fortunate enough to have both tools but given only one, I would have to go with the acute angled gouge. If one of those problem situations did come up, all I would have to do is regrind my tool to satisfy the situation. Of course, the downside of this is that you keep grinding your tool back and forth, which makes it shorter and soon you have to buy a new one. So…it's six of one, half dozen of the other.

This is a 9/16" **shallow gouge**. It is not meant for bowl turning, but I use it quite frequently for detailing and shear cutting. The wings are pulled back quite severely and the tip is radiused smaller than a normal fingernail grind. It is also fitted with a longer bowl type handle, even though it is basically a spindle gouge. The reason for the long handle is that it lies up against my thigh and helps dampen vibrations and balance the tool. At times it is even laid under my arm to use one-handed.

The tool in its working position is just right of the point. As you can see, it takes a very fine cut. With the smaller radiused point I feel that it functions similarly to a much smaller tool (like a 1/4" bowl gouge) but still has strength. My feeling is that a smaller gouge presents less cutting surface, so at times it does a much better job of cutting some grain than a larger gouge. The minuses are that a smaller gouge has a tendency to vibrate and also that with a smaller tool you have less bevel riding, leading to a tendency to develop ridges and inconsistencies due to tool movement. It all boils down to the turner's ability. Also, this is not meant as a tool to remove large amounts of wood. It is more of a finesse tool.

Another nice factor of this tool is the way it shear cuts. Being shallow, and with the ears or wings pulled way back, it presents a flatter cutting edge. Again, other tools would probably accomplish the same shear cut, but sometimes—for some unknown reason—I can cut much more cleanly with this tool on a given piece of wood than with others. My imagination? I don't think so. It's worked too many times for me. Besides, as I said before—I am a tool junkie.

Here is a 3/8" **spindle gouge**. It is not necessarily thought of as a bowl tool, but I use it as a detailing tool. Given one tool in my kit bag, this would be it. I believe I can do just about anything with a 3/8" spindle gouge, by regrinding it to meet the situation.

This smaller gouge can get into places that you cannot possibly get to with a larger tool. I use it a lot for detailing around the foot and rim of a bowl. For example, if I put a bead on a bowl—whether at the foot or the side or wherever—this is the tool I grab. At times I even use it to shear cut, not necessarily because it does anything different than the other tools, but because it happens to be in my hand at the time. I've even pulled slivers out with it.

This is a **heavy scraper**. It is short with heavily radiused bottom edges and ground to a scraper contour. The two sides make it usable left or right.

When I use this tool, it is not in the normal scraping mode. I use it as a shear cut tool. What makes this any different than a gouge? Because it essentially has a straight cutting edge, I sometimes vary the angle that I approach the work from when I am using the scraper. Instead of 45 degrees, which is normal, I may put it at a much more inclined angle with much lighter pressure and work a problem area. It also will work a surface to create a smooth plane.

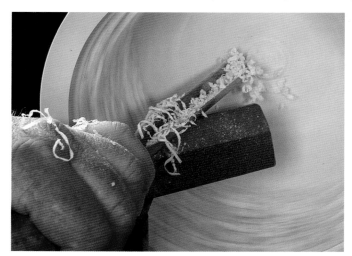

In these pictures, I am using the **acute angled bowl gouge**. This is our workhorse for clearing out the inside of a bowl. This particular grind will be good from the rim to the very bottom of most bowls. As you can see, the bevel will still rub across the bottom without the tool fouling out on the rim of the bowl.

The tool on the left is the 30 degree gouge. As you can see, the edge of that gouge is fouling out against the bowl and the bevel is off of the surface. This would be toying with disaster as nothing is supporting the bevel, which controls the cutting edge during the cut. The acute angle gouge, however, is nowhere near the edge of the bowl and the bevel is still in contact with the bottom of the bowl.

A way around this problem is to take your gouge and roll it on its side so the flutes are 90 degrees to vertical.

The 30 degree gouge does a nice job of cutting a clean surface. It would be good part of the way down the bowl, before fouling out and lifting the bevel. Occasionally, if you are working on a deep bowl, this gouge may cut the top of the bowl better than the acute gouge. You would still need the acute gouge to finish the bottom of the bowl, however. Again, it's one of those things that is not always necessary but at times works better than something else.

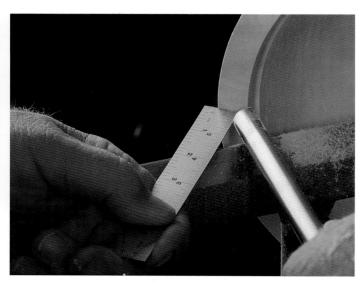

You also want your bevel 90 degrees to the surface.

I am sure anyone who has turned bowls has at some time had the gouge skate across the surface of the rim when trying to start a cut on the inside of the bowl. The reason for this frustrating mistake is that the tool is presented to the work with no support for the bevel. As the cutting edge touches the wood, the edge bites in and, with nothing to hold it, scoots across the surface uncontrolled. This normally damages the bowl according to the amount of pressure applied to the tool (i.e., as Newton said, for every action there is an equal and opposite reaction), as well as significantly damaging your ego.

If you have your tool on its side with the flutes 90 degrees to vertical, the bevel 90 degrees to the surface, and the tool at center line parallel to the lathe, it won't cut. It will, however, make a slight indentation that will support the cutting edge when you roll over the tool.

Rolling over your tool and dropping the handle to put the cutting edge into proper position, all in one smooth movement, uses the edge of that scored indentation to support the bevel. A little practice will build your confidence. Another aspect to remember and practice is that you should approach this cut using a secure grip, but not one that is too heavy handed. The harder you resist, the more damage is done if you do make a mistake. I understand this goes against the grain of usual thinking, but a "white knuckle grip" has no place in turning. By the way, this way of starting a gouge is not limited to bowls. It's a way of life in turning wood.

This is a **heavy radiused scraper**. Many people have a difficult time cutting the inside of the bowl's bottom cleanly. At the very center of the bottom, they often end up with a high spot or at times a low spot, a belly button (innies or outies). In addition, the bowl is turning considerably slower at the center than it is at the outer diameter, which makes for a less than desirable cutting action. Many turners push the tool through this area too fast rather than slowing down the cut. This then becomes a surface in need of help. This is where the heavy scraper can be used to clean up the very bottom and blend it into the side of the bowl.

When using the scraper, the positioning is at center line or slightly below. If you come in with an above center line attitude, and a catch is made, the tool is pulled down and levered into the wood. At center line, if a catch is made, there is nothing below it so the tool will kick away from the surface, creating much less damage. You cannot use the full contour of the scraper, as the cutting surface would be too great and present you with all kinds of problems—chattering, catching, and so forth. We do want the radiused shape of the tool to come somewhere close to the contours of the bowl, to make it easy to blend, but we only use a small part of it. Again, this is a light cut. It's not meant to move a lot of material—that's what a gouge is for.

Sometimes you will have ripples or non-uniform cutting on the sides of the bowl. In such situations, I stand my radiused scraper on an approximately 45 degree angle and make a shear cut. This helps smooth out any ripples, bumps, and imperfections prior to sanding. If you tried to do this in a normal scraping mode, chances are you would set up a very bad vibration and catch (given that the bowl is getting thin at this point). I also use my hand on the outside of a bowl to help dampen any vibrations. Remember that using the radiused scraper in this way is meant to enhance the surface, not to remove a lot of stock.

Chucks

Shown here are the chucks that I normally use for turning bowls. There are a ton of them on the market, but these seem to be my favorites. I believe a good chuck should be solid and carry a good weight, which acts as a flywheel; be shielded from dust and dirt; and be user friendly. No matter what chuck you get, learning the various ways of using it will provide you with the greatest benefit.

Faceplate. Probably the most versatile means of holding on a lathe. A faceplate and a scrap block will handle just about any situation that arises.

Screw chuck. Very similar to a faceplate, but has one very sharp thread cutting screw in the center. With this we can hold the work directly on it or use it with a scrap block.

Vicmarc™ 3 1/2" key operated chuck with standard jaws. I like this chuck as it is small in size, very solid, and key operated. I am not a fan of lever operated chucks as I prefer to be able to use one hand to place the work piece and the other hand to lock it down. There are various jaws available for this chuck. I normally use this set most of the time. My other chucks cover other situations. Another nice feature of this chuck is that it has an insert that can be replaced with various thread patterns to adapt to just about any lathe. Being small in size, this chuck is easy to work around but will still do a larger work piece.

Axminster™ key operated chuck with 4" dovetail jaws. These jaws have dovetails internally and externally. I normally use them externally. There are various smaller sizes available as well.

Axminster™ key operated chuck with gripper jaws. These are designed for holding relatively large diameters. With the depth of the jaws they also hold pieces such as hollow forms or vases. Also, the jaws have a dovetail at the top that can be used as an expanding chuck.

Axminster™ key operated chuck with regular jaws. These jaws will hold a square or round diameter piece. The holding power is not near as much as say the gripper jaws, on account of there is less jaw in contact with the work. But for grabbing a 2 x 2 etc., they excel.

Axminster™ key operated chuck with O'Donnell jaws. These jaws are designed to give access around the jaws for close in tool work. They also come in 1 1/2" and 2" sizes. The end of the jaws have internal and external dovetails. They are nice for small bowls, for expanding grips.

The Axminster™ chuck is probably the ultimate in chucks. It is based on a machine chuck and its weight reflects this. The best feature of this chuck is its ability to change jaws easily and swiftly. Changing jaws is nothing more than opening the chuck until the jaws are released from their slides, putting in another set, and closing the chuck. Very convenient. The chuck also has a replaceable backing plate, which comes in various thread sizes. So if you change lathes, your chuck can go with you. This chuck has many more types of jaws available than I've shown here. The downside of this chuck and all the various jaws and jaw slides is that the cost has become close to that of a decent used car.

Equipment

Every man is proud of his shop and I am no different. The normal lament is that there is not enough room…I second it! My shop happens to be in my basement. It has its good points and bad. It is warm in the winter and cool in the summer due to being heated and air-conditioned, which is necessary in my area. It is also dry, which protects my lathes and tools from rust. During the summer I also run a dehumidifier. The downsides are stairs and having a dusty hobby in the house. Carrying half logs down the stairs and bags of shavings up becomes a chore. I do have an additional band saw in my garage where I am able to saw out blanks and leave the scrap and mess out of the house. Being in the garage keeps it contained where I can easily clean it up.

The dust aspect in the shop can be a problem. To help this situation, I have installed a 1-1/2 horsepower dust collection system. I built a soundproof closet large enough to contain the dust collector and installed a full size door to provide easy access for cleaning it. It has a baffle that returns the air back into the shop. I installed four 5" drops with gates in strategically placed locations in my shop. I have also installed a remote switch system and I carry the transponder in my shop coat pocket. Since doing this, I run the collector more, where before I hesitated to because of the noise it made. Silence can be golden.

I have a collection of five lathes. The main reason being, I like lathes. My armada of lathes consists of a 20" Harrison Graduate™ shortbed, a 9" Vicmarc™ 100 mini lathe, a 16" Vicmarc™ 200 longbed, a 24" Vicmarc™ 300 shortbed and a Carbatec™, which is also a mini. The three large lathes all have variable speed motors. The lathe that I use most is the 16" Vicmarc, because it is user friendly and it handles the majority of my turning projects. The 24" Vicmarc is used mainly for bowls or large projects. The Vicmarc 100 mini is used for pens and small projects and at times is transported when I do demonstrations. The Harrison Graduate is seldom used but is still a favorite. That leaves the Carbatec, which at this time does nothing but collect dust but still holds a tender spot in my heart. It is hard to get rid of old friends.

If I could only have one lathe, I would choose my 16" longbed. I believe if you only own one lathe, it should definitely be a longbed rather than a shortbed. Not only will it handle longer spindles, but you can also slide the tailstock to the end of the lathe, getting it out of the way, and still have room to work at the headstock. With a shortbed lathe, you end up having to remove the tailstock when working on a bowl. I am getting too old to be continually picking up that tailstock.

This is my main turning area. In front of each lathe I have a cushioned mat, which I consider a necessity. Behind each lathe is a gate to the dust collector. I also have plenty of lighting.

Note the door for the dust collector in the right hand corner.

This is the closet housing my dust collector. Also note the grinder just outside the door. I find grinders are normally too low to suit me. I have therefore built mine up to accommodate my height. This allows me to grind in an upright position and improves my visibility. Grinders are very necessary for sharp tools—why not make them user friendly as well?

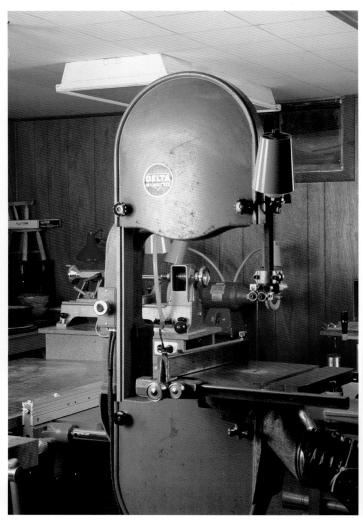

I consider the band saw to be a companion to the lathe. You can saw out blanks, make square blanks round, plus accomplish a multitude of odds jobs that are always cropping up. A while back I called the company for repair parts. When the girl who answered asked me for a model number, I told her there wasn't one. She said, "Huh, I don't suppose it has a part number either!" I said yes it did and gave it to her. She replied, "Wow, this saw was made in May of 1952." I replied "That makes sense as I received the saw for Christmas in 1952." Good tools, if taken care of, will last a lifetime.

A drill press is a necessary tool in my shop. I use mine continually. I would find it difficult to get along without it.

The Basic Bowl

I am going to assume that the individual reading this book has never turned a green wood bowl before and has no idea how to cut or work with green wood. So let's start differently than most books and use a dimensional blank for the first bowl, expanding our knowledge as we go.

For someone just starting to turn, the first bowl will probably be a dimensional blank. In other words, it will probably have been bought from a wood supplier or cut from dimensioned lumber that was lying around. The main reason for turning this bowl is to establish methods of getting a firm hold on the blank, as mounting and remounting it accurately seems to bewilder many turners. I will be turning the entire bowl from start to finish. Though many detailed situations are covered in this project, many additional details not applicable at this stage will be covered in other sections of the book.

If the blank has been purchased, it will probably be relatively dry; if it has been cut from dimensioned lumber, it will probably have been kiln dried. The blank I am using is a piece of slightly figured walnut that I have had for years and that I am sure is quite dry. With this piece, drying will not be a problem—we will be able to do the bowl from start to finish without a drying period. The initial step of laying out the blank involves determining where the figure will end up in the bowl. If the figure is uniform throughout the blank, layout is simple. If the figure is more dominant on one surface than another, however, I would put the figured surface to the bottom of the bowl. Not doing so is a classic mistake made by the novice. His first belief is that all the figure must be on the top of the bowl where it shows. In reality, this will all be cut away as the bowl is hollowed out, leaving all that beautiful figure on the floor in the form of shavings. By orientating it so that the figure is on the bottom of the piece, the majority of it will remain when the bowl is completed. Here I have used a pair of dividers to find the center of the blank and drawn a circle, which will become the diameter of my bowl.

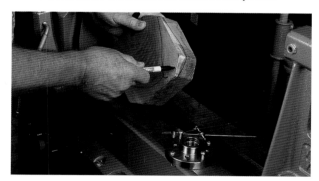

My usual way of developing a form utilizes the entire blank if possible. I find it difficult to waste wood needlessly—it is hard enough to get good usable wood without throwing part of it away. Of course, there are times when this does not hold true. A blank may be highly figured on one side or on the majority, but

have a bland area that could be eliminated by making a smaller bowl. This would give the entire bowl fancier figure and eliminate the plain area. On this particular blank, you can see that there is sapwood on one side, which I have marked for clarity. Since I do not care to have this on the top edge of the bowl, I will orient it so it is on the bottom—which unfortunately goes against our best grain in the bottom. Life is not always fair but this will produce the best bowl.

I am aware that a first time bowl turner may not have a three or four jaw chuck. So for this bowl, I will use a face plate and scrap block. Face plates come with every lathe so chances are one will be available. I consider scrap blocks used with a face plate the most universal means of holding things on a lathe. They are not always the fastest or most convenient, but will handle about anything you can throw at them. Another thing I like about scrap blocks is that when using a figured blank such as this one, they help prevent me from losing any more of the wood than is necessary. In other words, if I needed to cut a tenon to hold for a chuck in a contraction mode, I would have to reduce the thickness of the blank. Similarly, if I cut a recess for a chuck with expanding jaws, I would be limited on the diameter of the finished bowl's foot. Another plus for the novice turner is that a face plate and decent screws will probably have a better grip than some chucks (depending on jaws used), making things a little safer.

I have already trimmed the waste on the band saw and we now want to center the face plate to the blank. The easiest way is to take a pair of dividers and find the diameter of the face plate.

Using the same center mark that you scribed the bowl diameter with, mark the face plate diameter. This will give you a witness line with which to center the face plate on the blank. I have marked mine in black here for visual purposes.

The screws on my face plate are protruding approximately 5/8". Since this is a small blank (roughly 7" diameter by 2 1/4") and the wood is dry, this will be quite adequate. If the wood were larger and green, longer screws would be needed to obtain more holding power. If the piece is end grain or punky, you would want to put even more screws in if your face plate will accept them. If you are going to err, err on the safe side.

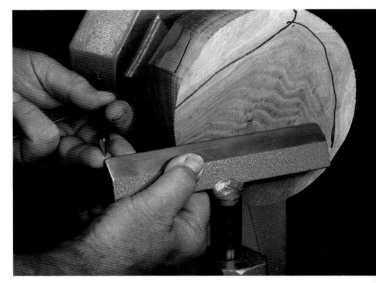

Another point about screws: I like to use a screw that fills the hole in the face plate. If you use smaller diameter screws than the faceplate holes and if you then make a catch or stress the blank during turning, the screws could shift to one side of the hole in the face plate and make your work piece off center. Fill those holes! As far as type of screws, I like sheet metal screws. To me, dry wall screws are a no-no. Normally they are too small in diameter and are hard, which makes them brittle. The sheet metal screws will normally drill and cut their own threads, especially in green wood. When using some of the hardwoods, you may want to drill pilot holes using the holes in the face plate to locate them, so as not to split or crack any of the wood around the hole. Wood screws are fine, but normally demand a pilot hole. Another thing I like is a Robertson or square drive screw. Phillip's head or slot head screws always seem to cam out on me (damage the driving surface). In contrast, the square drive screws seem to provide the best torque without slippage, allowing me to use them over and over.

Always make sure your tool rest is clean and smooth. If it has a bunch of nicks, dents, or anything that can catch the chisel or tool you are using, it will leave a mark in the surface of the work as you go over it. I normally hit mine on a belt sander as often as necessary or use a mill file when a sander is not available. I have even been forced during demonstrations to use sandpaper and a block of wood. It is also very helpful to radius off the very outside edges of the corners, where my pencil is pointing. Inevitably these are sticking out or protruding from the lathe as you work or pass by them, and they seem to have a magnetic attraction towards skin.

I normally use a variable speed drill with a square drive bit to drive the screws. (A hand held screwdriver will do everything the drill will, but you'll need more time and end up with calluses.) Using the witness line you drew previously, center the faceplate and carefully drive in your screws.

Using a 3/8" spindle gouge, I am starting to clean up the base.

I have surfaced the very bottom and made it flat. This will provide a glue surface for our scrap block.

Here is a scrap block that I have surfaced in preparation for gluing. A scrap block is exactly what it sounds like—an expendable piece of wood that can be cut away without remorse to allow clearance for your tools. I usually use woods such as poplar, soft maple, or anything else that's in my scrap bin, walnut included. I do not like pine, as it is too soft. The scrap block should be relatively thin in order to keep the work piece close to your faceplate or chuck. A 4" thick scrap block would probably be prone to setting up vibrations, while a 1" thick block would not. Basically, keep your scrap block only as thick as necessary so that your screws do not go all the way through and damage the surface on the opposite side, which is the work piece. Just common sense.

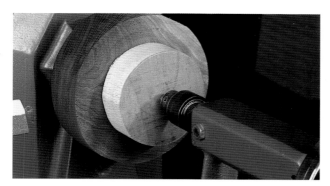

If you are not sure of your eye or have trouble centering things, probably the best way to center the scrap block would be to bring up your tailstock and—using your live center in the hole that you used to scribe the diameter of the scrap block (when you cut it out)—advance the tailstock and press both blocks together to make sure the surfaces are flat and provide a good gluing surface. The lathe in this step is nothing more than a large centering clamp. Gluing can be done in several ways. My preference is to use medium density cyanoacrylate glue because of its speed and ease of use. It sets up immediately and allows me to continue without a wait. On the adverse side, time and cyanoacrylate wait for no man…if you make a mistake or don't move fast enough you're cooked. White or yellow glues can also be used, but you have the time factor to consider: drying time is hours—versus seconds with the cyanoacrylate. However, if you are finishing for the day and can allow the white or yellow glue to cure overnight, it will do everything that cyanoacrylate does.

Using a pair of calipers, find the diameter of your face plate.

Clean up the diameter of the scrap block.

Using the calipers with which you established the faceplate diameter, take a parting tool and transfer that diameter to the scrap block. When we true up the scrap block to this diameter, it will give us a visual and mechanical way of centering the faceplate back to the scrap block when the bowl is turned around.

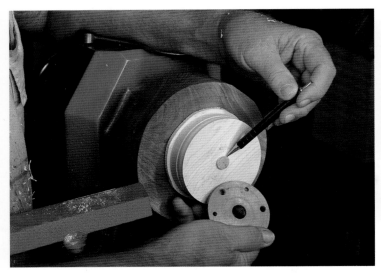

One of the simplest and most accurate ways of locating a faceplate to a scrap block that is already on the lathe is to make a tenon and flat surface that mates to the faceplate surface, as I've done here. As you can see, there is a hole in the center of this workpiece…

…which just presses over the tenon snugly. If done accurately, this will give a perfect alignment. Just put in your screws and reverse the faceplate.

OK, so what if your faceplate does not have a center hole? This is too good of a setup to quit on. Make a recess that the outside of the face plate fits into…

… and *voila*, we have a centered faceplate again. I suggest you file both of these methods away in your head, as they are very versatile in all facets of woodturning when you need to center an object.

For those of you fortunate enough to have a chuck (which, as you can see, I am), this would be the time to take your scrap block and turn it to whatever diameter you need to accommodate your chuck. But since we started out doing this for the individual who does *not* have all of the conveniences, I am going to continue on with the most basic method—the faceplate.

Remove the bowl and faceplate from the lathe, then remove the faceplate from the bowl blank. Reverse and mount the faceplate on the scrap block. Since some people have only one faceplate and would not be able to locate a second faceplate to the scrap block with a tenon or recess, we are using our set diameter—which should be the same as our faceplate—to locate it. This is not the most perfect setup, but with care will still be within the realm of concentricity. It is also the reason I did not turn any of the outside of the bowl before fitting the faceplate to the scrap block.

Using a bowl gouge, start truing up the outside of your work piece. My speed is probably a "guesstimation" of 1100-1200 rpm. You want to have enough speed to cut decently but not so much that it causes you problems, such as vibration, burning, etc. Too much speed also becomes dangerous. Always check for cracks, loose knots, or anything else that could impair your safety. If you are going to err, err on the slow side.

I am reducing the bottom of the bowl and scrap block to start developing a form. On this particular bowl, my faceplate is quite large. With a smaller one, the base of the bowl would have been much more accessible. But we are going under the assumption that we only have one faceplate and we are going to have to back ourselves out of the proverbial hole to make things work. As you reduce the scrap block, keep in mind that you have screws through the faceplate holding it on. They have a very distinct way of ruining a cutting edge on your tools if you forget about them.

I am using a 3/8" spindle gouge to cut some of my scrap block away. This will provide me with access to the foot area of the bowl and help me work towards the shape of the bowl.

Using the 3/8" spindle gouge in a shear cut mode, which is about on a 45 degree angle, pulling uphill, smooth out your shape. This is not a riding the bevel cut, it is a shear cut. When I used the bowl gouge, I was cutting in a bevel rubbing mode. Taking light cuts, establish your form. Do not just use your arms when you turn, use your entire body, as your movements will be much smoother. If you use just your arms to move the tool, your movements will become jerky and this will be reflected in the finished surface. There are numerous ways to work the outside surface of the bowl, but these will be discussed on another bowl of larger proportions where you will be able to see them better. On this small bowl, our 3/8" spindle gouge will do the job adequately as long as it is kept sharp.

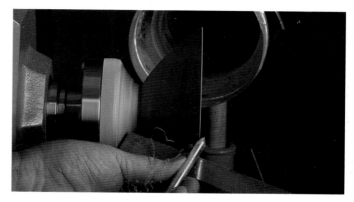

Every once in a while, carefully knock the sharp edge off the very rim—not a lot, just enough to turn it into a blunt edge instead of a sharp meat saw. That sharp edge, whether it be the edge of a bowl or a shoulder of any part of a sharp rotating surface, can really cut. Once you've experienced the result of not taking this precaution, you will wish you had listened to my advice. Best is not to have this experience at all.

Using a bowl gouge, make smooth even cuts to start hollowing out the inside. Remember, the main purpose of this small bowl is to illustrate and practice the basic methods of setup using a faceplate and scrap block, as well as, to show how (using a dimensioned blank) we are not going to waste any of the wood in thickness. As noted earlier, I am going to discuss different cutting methods for the outside of the bowl later. Ditto for the inside. However, we do need to address some basic cuts now.

Continued work on hollowing out the bowl.

Using a pair of double ended calipers, check to see if your wall is a uniform thickness from top to bottom. If it is not, make it so.

Using a 3/8" spindle gouge, I am angling the rim, which will produce shadows. (I don't like a flat rim.) It is important to do this before you complete the hollowing out as the extra stock lends strength and support.

Using a heavy flat round nosed scraper at center line or slightly below, clean up the very bottom of the bowl. Use a light touch.

Notice how my hand is cupping the outside of the bowl to help dampen any vibrations. The pressure that I am applying on the outside of the bowl is equal to the pressure I am applying with the gouge. Light.

At times, you may have ridges or a bad mark between the bottom and the side wall—using the tool in a scraping position at such times will set up a vibration due to thin walls. By rolling the scraper up on its side to approximately a 45 degree angle and backing up the bowl with your hand to dampen any vibrations, you can lightly shear some of those imperfections out prior to sanding. Again, this is a light, delicate cut. It is not meant to move a lot of wood, it is meant to refine the surface.

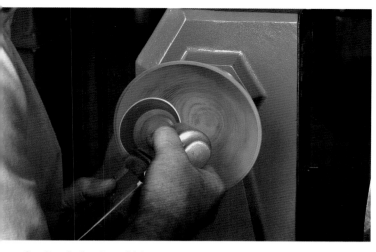

Sanding the bowl out. Make sure your grit is coarse enough to clean up any imperfections (see page 38 for additional information on sanding).

Immediately take 0000 steel wool and the oil of your choice and apply to the surface. Apply the oil with a scrubbing action. This takes most of the Deft™ off the surface and leaves it in the pores, but gives you an oil finish. I always do this with the lathe stopped, so as not to scratch the surface with concentric rings.

Apply a little coat of Deft™ and keep any drying spots wet.

Wipe down the surface and make sure it looks the way you want it to, as it is easier to sand missed scratches while the bowl is still on the lathe rather than after it has been removed.

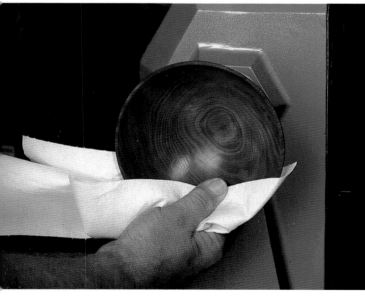

With the lathe stopped, use a paper towel to wipe off the excess finish.

Take a parting tool and cut the scrap block behind the bowl. Leave a small amount of the scrap block on the bowl so as not to damage the bowl—we will remove this when we finish the bottom. As your diameter gets close to being parted off, you can use a small saw to cut the rest with the lathe stopped. Or, if you cut a small enough diameter, the tenon can be popped off, also with the lathe stopped. Just make sure when you go to pop it off you are not trying to pop it off against the end grain. Face grain separates much easier.

Mount a piece of scrap on the faceplate. It should be larger than the rim diameter of the bowl as it is going to be a jam chuck to reverse the bowl. I am using a piece of scrap poplar, but I prefer MDF (medium density fiberboard). Using a spindle gouge, lightly true up the diameter.

When cutting the rebate, you want the outside wall to be parallel to the axis of the lathe. An easy way to establish this is to line your tool up with the bed of the lathe. The way this particular jam chuck works is the largest diameter of the rim is being held by a friction tight fit. The face of the rim is also in contact with the bottom of the rebate. This is important as it adds stability to keep the bowl from rocking, which could dislodge it.

Using a parting tool, start to cut a rebate for the rim of the bowl. Work carefully, as the closeness of the jam chuck is going to hold and drive your bowl. I am using my eye to determine the diameter I need. If you feel more comfortable, you can mark the diameter out first, but be sure to cut it undersize.

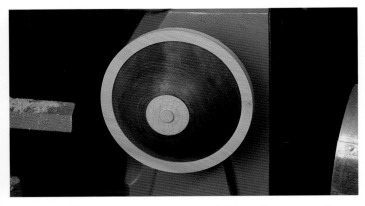

When your rebate is the correct size, your bowl will actually snap in and be held in place. The depth of the rebate need only be slightly deeper than the widest point on the rim—excessive depth will not hold any better. If for some reason your rebate is too large and the bowl will not hold, you could wrap the edge with tape or use a paper towel over the opening and jam the bowl into it.

Checking the fit. We need to cut it larger.

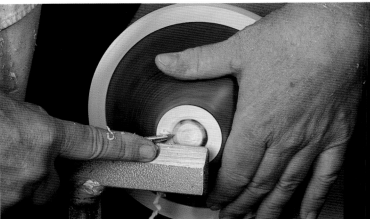

I am using a small 1/4" gouge to clean off the scrap from the bottom of the bowl, making my cuts in the direction of the headstock. I'm using my hand as a safety, just to hold it in. If you have difficulty with this, an alternative would be to bring the tailstock up lightly and leave a small tenon where the point contacts the base to help hold the bowl in the chuck. This could be cut away at the very end or cut off by hand. Tape or plastic twine wrapped around the bowl body and jam chuck will also work.

If you are a normal human being, at some point or another you will probably forget to check the thickness of the bowl at the base. With the jam chuck method, you can actually take the bowl out, check it, return it to the same position, and still have it concentric. This is because the bowl is being held in with a friction fit by the outer diameter of the rim, so even if your bowl has gone out of round the jam chuck will force it back into being concentric.

Another reason I like using a scrap block is that I can alter the diameter of the bowl's foot. If using a chuck with expanding jaws, I would have to cut a recess for the chuck jaws. The size of the recess may limit me from making a smaller foot if I so desire. In this case, I think it should be a little more delicate on this thin bowl so I am reducing it. This also means that I have to reform the base of the bowl and blend it into the finished area.

Blending the bottom of the bowl into the recut foot.

Undercutting the bottom of the foot. This step finishes the bottom of the bowl, eliminating any indication of how it was held. If the bowl later warps, running it across a piece of sandpaper on a flat surface will flatten the outer rim of the foot easily, making it stable again.

I like to take a small gouge and turn a small bead in the recess. This has become kind of my signature.

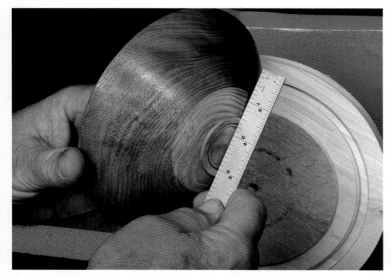

We've turned the bottom and the contour matches the inside of the bowl.

Sand the bottom of the foot as well as the bottom of the bowl where it was blended to the foot.

Finish using the same steps described previously.

The finished bowl. This may have seemed like the hard way to get to the end result, but remember we were showing how to achieve this without using anything but a faceplate and scrap. Plus, we utilized the total thickness of our blank.

Green Wood Harvesting

To make larger and especially deeper bowls, material becomes a problem. Dimensional lumber is rare to find in 3" to 4" thickness and is normally expensive. To accommodate our turning needs, we need to turn green wood, as larger sizes can be obtained at minimal cost.

Occasionally you may get a hold of a log, whether it be from a tree service, neighbor's yard, or whatever. Proper handling of such wood is foreign to most new turners. The sooner you work the green wood, the less waste (e.g., cracking or checking) you will have. If you are planning to take a lot of wood, you are going to have to protect it until you can get time to work it. By not protecting the wood or by cutting it haphazardly, a lot of waste and mediocre results will occur.

Although I generally use a gas chain saw for rough cutting, an electric chain saw is much more "neighbor friendly." The first step in working the log is to cut it into sections slightly longer than the diameter, providing I am going to work them right away—otherwise, leave excess materials on the ends. The next step is to split the log lengthwise right down the pith. After you have split the log, anything that remains can be used as material. There are various ways of laying out bowl blanks, which I will discuss in this section.

If there will be a period of time before you can work the piece, seal the ends with green wood sealer or paint them with latex paint to retard the drying process. I normally store my logs in the shade and out of the wind, if possible, as wind accelerates the drying process. Leave the bark on as it too will retard drying. If you have only some small branch wood or a couple of small pieces of trunk, put them in a plastic bag—again, this will stop the drying process by not allowing the passage of air, which would promote drying. Note that a piece left in a plastic bag too long will sweat, which causes discoloration and occasionally spalting. Sometimes, if I rough turn a piece of work that has light spalting in it, I will throw some of the spalted shavings into a plastic bag along with the bowl and hope for additional spalting.

If you look at where I am pointing to the pith with my pencil, you will see some small circular growth ring patterns right on the edge of the rim. These are subject to cracking during the drying process and not having a lot of strength afterwards. By repositioning the bowl (i.e., the red line), we can eliminate these suspect areas and end up with a better result. While this may take an extra saw cut, it may also save an inch or two on the depth of your bowl by its not cracking in the suspect area.

I have laid out the end of this log showing how to get the largest bowl out of the log. As you can see, the pith was not exactly in the center of this log. Normally the pith is much more centered than this one, which makes for more uniform looking bowls. But this one will still provide a nice, deep bowl. Probably most people, having made the saw cut, would lay the bowl out to that cut. In other words, look at the black line, which is square to the cut. This would work, but there is a better way on this particular piece.

Another option for this log would be to make a natural edge bowl out of it. Layout would be as you see here. Still another option, if you run into knots or cracks or any imperfections that would be undesirable in a bowl, is to make turning squares out of a log. Another thing that I often do, especially when I come across pieces that are too small for bowls but are highly figured or desirable wood, is to cut out weed pot or clock material, seal the pieces, throw them aside, and forget about them. Sooner or later, I will need a piece of say 3 or 4" dry material and I normally have some handy. This is just a good way of utilizing what some people would throw away or burn in their fireplace.

Roughing Out a Bowl

Starting to clean up the blank. I am using my 30 degree bowl gouge primarily because I like it. Notice that I do not have a death grip on the tool, but I am holding it firmly with the tool handle against my thigh. This is just for stability because part of the time you will be cutting air, given that the piece is not yet round.

Many turners are under the belief that the bowl gouge is supposed to be positioned at center line during the cut. This would create a scrape rather than a cut. To start a cut, the gouge is positioned above center, riding on the heel or back of the bevel, which holds the cutting edge slightly above the surface to be cut. Carefully and slowly pull back the tool and raise the handle in one smooth movement. As the cutting edge begins to cut, that's the optimum angle. Raising the handle slightly and advancing it forward will deepen the cut. Rolling or changing the directional angle may be necessary to locate the sweet spot. This procedure is not limited to bowls and is used with most tools with the exception of scrapers. Scrapers are used at center line or just a tad below.

This is a section of mesquite that we are going to rough out for a bowl. The reason we are going to rough it out is that in its solid form, a half log, it would take forever to dry. With large logs, the center probably never would dry. By turning the walls to a uniform thickness, such as an inch, we will speed up the drying period considerably. A good rule of thumb is that air drying equals one year per inch thickness.

I am going to make the largest bowl I can out of this block by putting my faceplate to the center or pith area of the blank. I am using a faceplate because it gives me a lot of strength. A screw chuck would also work. Before you start, check the piece out completely to ensure your own personal safety. Notice the bark on the piece and check to make sure it is not loose. If it is, get rid of it rather than letting it fly haphazardly around your shop. Remember, this is an out of balance piece and you have no idea what it's going to do when you turn the lathe on. Set your speed low. It's always easier to increase the speed than to try and remount the bowl after it has come off the lathe. It may sound elementary, but also check for cracks. A crack could go the length of the long grain and separate the blank into two pieces as you are working on it. In addition, some woods are sopping wet when you go to rough turn them. I normally hang a plastic drop cloth from ceiling to floor between my lathe and the rest of my shop. This precaution prevents the wet shavings and moisture from being thrown on my machines and tools. This can be very important, as I've had a puddle of sap laying on the floor in line with the turnings and headstock. Yes, you also get it on your clothes.

Green wood sure cuts easy.

Forming a tenon or foot on the bowl that can be grabbed in a chuck.

Taking a cut to make our basic shape.

I am going to be using a chuck to grip the tenon. Part of the chuck's grip is contact with either the face or the base of the jaws. In other words, we will be compressing the diameter in the jaws and should contact either the base or the face of the jaws, which helps keep the bowl from deflecting. My chuck will probably have greater depth than the length of the tenon. Not wanting to lose any more of the height of the bowl than necessary, I have put a small flat on the base of the bowl, 90 degrees to the tenon, which will act as a stop against the face of my jaws. This will help give me support while I hollow out the inside. I used my 3/8" spindle gouge to do this.

Another thing that I always like to do on green wood turning is to leave a witness mark at the very center. I am using my 3/8" spindle gouge to leave a slight dimple. This will be used after drying to reposition the bowl for final turning. It is solely a convenience.

Our bowl is ready to be removed. Between my fingers is an area that has not been cleaned up, but a light cut would do it. This will be cleaned up after drying, when it is remounted.

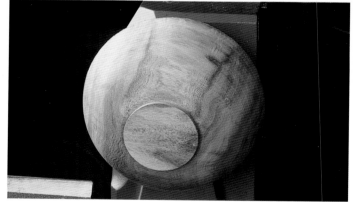

Notice that there is still some sapwood as well as a small spot on a corner of the tenon that have not cleaned up. However, I see no reason to further reduce the bowl before drying, just to eliminate these little blemishes. As the bowl dries, it will warp and distort and chances are these areas will be cleaned up along with the rest of the bowl later. At this point, I also like to create a "unisex" shape (i.e., no ogees, decorative beads, etc.), unless the piece dictates differently. A unisex shape allows for many design variations after drying. What I thought might be nice today may look very different two years from now. Even your style may change drastically, so don't hinder yourself by getting too specific now.

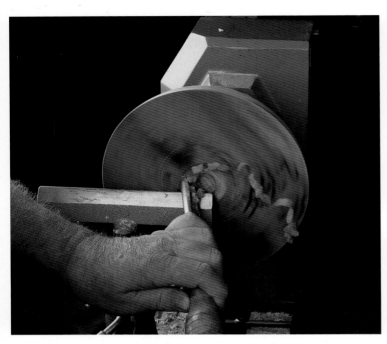

I have put my four jaw chuck on the lathe and grabbed the tenon. The flat at the top of the tenon is tight against the face of the jaws. This gives me the best stability I can. Using my acute angled bowl gouge, I am starting to hollow out the inside of the bowl.

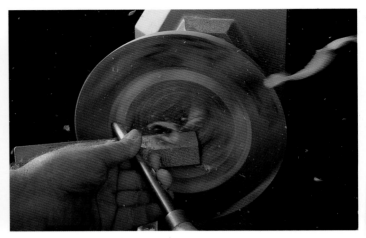

Continuing to get rid of excess material.

Green wood cuts very easily so I normally hollow out the bowl aggressively.

A clean cut on the inside of a bowl is actually performed in the shape of an arc. This line shows the path that my tool takes.

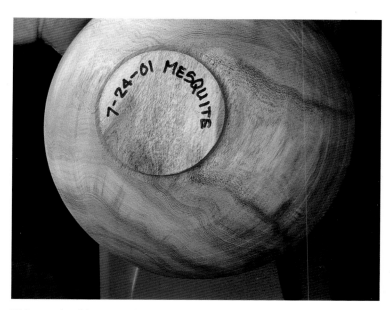

The second line is parallel to the tool rest. You *can* cut the bowl straight across at the tool rest height, but you will probably end up with torn grain or an unsatisfactory cut. This is caused by the cutting edge and bevel not being in its optimum cutting position. To start a cut inside a bowl with the gouge, start by positioning the heel of the gouge above center line. If done properly, it won't cut, as the heel is holding the cutting edge above the surface. Slowly pull your tool back and raise the handle. The cutting edge will then start to cut. This is the optimum angle. Raise the handle and advance the tool forward to obtain the depth of the cut. You may have to roll or change the position of the tool to find the sweet spot. Make your cut. When the bevel and cutting edge are riding right, they will present a curved path ending at the exact center of the bowl. The shape of the bowl dictates the shape of the arc. With practice, you will learn the proper feel and sound of the cut and the appearance of the shavings. When you apply these, along with the arc, you will no doubt be pleasantly surprised.

With a marker, I have noted the date and type of wood on the bottom. This ensures that I know when I did it and what it is. Mesquite is very obvious, but you may do a piece in some unusual species and, after a year or two of drying, you may forget what it was. If there are any knots I hit them now with some thin cyanoacrylate (hoping to avoid radial cracking of the knot) and then paint the entire bowl with a coat of green wood sealer.

The purpose of green wood sealer is to retard the drying. Wood is comprised of cells similar to a pack of straws, with the end grain corresponding to the hollow end of the straws. Naturally, if you were wicking moisture out, it would come out of the end grain much faster than the face grain. If it comes out too fast, however, the cells do not have a chance to shrink and cracking occurs. I coat my entire bowl, but you could speed up the process by only sealing the end grain and fancy grain (fancy grain is also very susceptible to cracking).

After applying the sealer, I like to leave the bowls on the floor for a few days to see how much they are going to move as the surface moisture starts to dry. If a crack does develop, normally in the heavier portion of the foot or tenon, I hit it with a shot of cyanoacrylate. If no cracks materialize in the first few days or week, I stack the bowls so air can pass through and let them dry. I normally have a supply of dried or drying bowls, so I am not concerned with the speed of drying.

This is definitely not the only way to dry bowls. If I were a production turner, turning many more bowls than I actually do, I would have to have a faster way to season my roughed out bowls. Many production turners make miniature kilns, but this is not applicable to the hobbyist. Another simple drying process would be to apply a heavy coat of paste wax instead of the green wood sealer. Still another method would be to place the bowl in a doubled brown paper bag, with no sealer. The thickness of the bags would retard air and moisture flow, working similarly to the sealers. The only problem is that this bag needs to be opened for a few hours on occasion to let moisture out. As the moisture dissipates during subsequent openings, the length of time the bag is open is increased. When the bulk of the moisture has dissipated, the bowl can be left out. Do not use plastic bags. No moisture will pass through them and they will sweat on the inside, which can stain the wood.

How do you know when the wood is dry? As stated before, I use time as the defining factor. In other words, after a year or two, normally less, my bowls are probably ready. As I

The roughed out bowl is now ready to come off. Mesquite, which is very stable, does not warp excessively as it dries. I have left the walls approximately 7/8" thick, and slightly heavier in the base. I left the base heavier to allow me to change patterns if I feel so inclined later on. If this had been apple, pear, or any of the woods that really go crazy while drying, I would have left the walls a little thicker to ensure material to work with after drying. Before taking the bowl off the lathe, the last thing you want to do is break the sharp edges on the rim. There are two reasons for this: one, the sharp edges can still be dangerous; and two, sharp distinct edges are more prone to cracks.

set them up to finish turning them, I normally feel the shavings. I know they are not sopping wet, but occasionally the shavings from a thick bowl may feel suspect. At this point, I just turn off all the sealer, which also reduces part of the excess wood, and set it aside to season a bit longer.

Many turners also weigh and date the piece upon completion of the rough out, which also helps with knowing when the piece is dry. After a couple of weeks, they weigh it and date it again. After a few samplings, a pattern will be established. As the wood dries, the weight will be less. Charted, this will produce a curve of weight loss, which, when it flattens out, means the piece is dry. Of course, the average humidity of your location will have a direct bearing on how quickly your piece dries.

What about moisture meters? I don't have one, don't really want one. If I were in a production mode I might use one, but do I really want to poke moisture meter pins into my bowl blanks? And yes, I know there are pinless moisture meters, but they need a flat surface. To put it bluntly, in this respect I am still a dinosaur.

A Roughing Out Tip

Woodturning is comprised of many little tricks. Here is one that can be very helpful in its place. It eliminates a couple of steps when you go to complete your dried bowl, as it provides you with a means of utilizing a four jaw chuck to hold your seasoned bowl.

I have put a piece of green (or unseasoned) mesquite on a screw chuck.

Start by removing waste material from the piece.

Clean up and face off what will be the bottom of the tenon.

Using a bowl gouge, I'm making the finished cut of our rough form. If the tenon will not contact the bottom of the jaws, we should have a 90 degree flat to the tenon that will contact the face of the jaws. Once this is done, we can turn the bowl around.

Not all things work out as you planned. Here was a beautiful piece of mesquite that was cut very close to the pith. I have had to lose part of the bowl's depth because of two cracks in the tight radial grain that is close to the pith. I'm just eliminating them. I guess I'm going to have a little smaller bowl than I intended.

Continuing to remove waste.

Hollowing out the bowl.

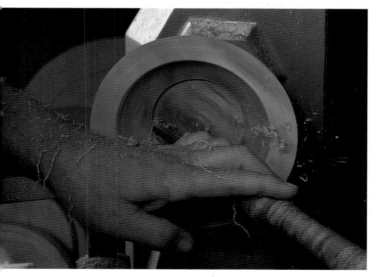

When you get close to the depth that you want to keep, cut a recess the size of your chuck into the inside bottom. For the sides, I used my 3/8" spindle gouge.

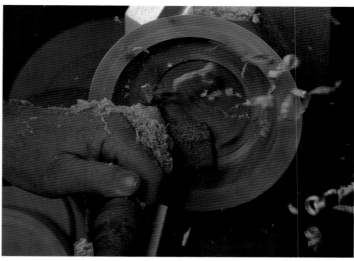

Take your walls to whatever thickness you intend, but don't cut out the recess.

This recess does not need to be fancy or super accurate, as it will warp as the bowl dries. I put a slight taper on my recess, kind of dovetail style. If you have flat jaws, it may be better just to have a 90 degree shoulder. This bowl is now completely roughed out, so we can date it, identify the species, and give it a coat of green wood sealer as described above (or use whatever means you decide for drying it).

When the time comes to use our dried blank, it will be very simple to grab it by the inner shoulders with the chuck in an expansion mode. Yes, I realize it might be warped. You may have to shift it slightly one way or the other to center it the best that you can. Once you have a good grip on it, however, you can turn the outside, the foot, put in a dovetail for an expansion chuck—whatever you want, including finishing it, all in one operation. When you turn it around, the holding area will be turned out along with the rest of the inside. You do need to take into consideration the depth between your jaws and the key that operates your chuck. If the bowl is too deep, you won't be able to operate your chuck, so keep this in mind when you go to cut your shoulder. This technique won't work with very deep bowls, but with shallow bowls it can be quite handy.

The Cherry Bowl

Well, two years have gone by fast…and here is a dry bowl. This is a piece of cherry that I roughed out two years ago. It should be dry. As you can see, it has shrunk 1/2" on the tangential grain. If it had not done this, it probably would have cracked. Also, this same shrinking occurred on the top of the rim, making it a crowned bowl. Our first step will be to remount this on the lathe and true up an area to hold it.

I have put a piece of MDF (that I have used as a jam chuck) on the lathe. This is going to align and drive the bowl. It should be somewhere close to the diameter but not at the very rim. Anything can be used as long as it is solid enough to support the bowl and some light turning. If I had left a shoulder on the inside of the bowl during the roughing out stage, I could now use my chuck to expand inside that shoulder and turn the entire bottom, minus the tailstock. However, I did not do that on this bowl, so that is why I am setting it up as I am.

Put the bowl over the scrap block and bring up the tailstock. Remember that witness mark we put in the foot of the roughed out bowl? I am using that witness mark as a center to locate the center of the foot. The live center has a cone tip in it. I prefer the cone tip over a 60 degree point as I can apply more pressure with the tailstock. (A 60 degree center would act as a wedge as you applied pressure and end up either burying itself or splitting the piece.) Before turning on the lathe, rotate the piece by hand and make sure everything clears, as you now are using an out of round blank. While you are doing this, pay attention to both the bowl and the foot. If it is excessively out of round in one direction, which occasionally happens, the live center tip can be repositioned to help correct this situation and make the bowl more concentric. In this case, the witness mark would not be used.

Make sure your speed has been slowed down on the lathe. Then, using a 3/8" spindle gouge, face off the very bottom of the foot.

Clean up the diameter of the foot and put a flat on the bottom of the bowl for the face of the jaws. Mount it in the chuck making sure the jaw faces are in contact with the flat on the bowl.

With my 30 degree gouge, I am using a pulling cut, which has the bevel rubbing on the surface. I'm pulling from the center towards the outside. I am doing this because I cannot get in the proper direction to keep a bevel on the surface. I could have used the more acute gouge, but this just feels more comfortable for me.

I now have room to swing the gouge around and make a proper cut.

Starting a cut with the gouge is difficult for some people to comprehend. If you notice, I am considerably above the center line and riding the bevel, but the cutting edge is still not in position. In other words, it's above the work and will not cut.

Drawing back and raising the handle brings the cutting edge into contact with the wood. When this happens, you will see the wood start to be cut. This is the angle that you want to maintain. The amount of forward and downward pressure that you apply is going to be in direct relation to the depth of the cut. Maintaining the cut is reminiscent of patting your head and rubbing your stomach at the same time. The only way you could maintain full bevel contact would be on a flat surface. We are cutting on a round surface, however, which means we have to alter our point of attack not only in height but by rolling and changing the angle of the gouge as it moves across the surface. Only a small portion of the bevel, behind the cutting edge, is in contact. Until you have conquered this move, making a smooth transitional curve will be difficult. Learn to listen, feel, hear, and sense when that wood is cutting cleanly and when it is not. When wood is not cutting cleanly, you can hear the tearing, you can feel it—nothing is functioning properly. Roll that gouge, raise it, lower it…find the "sweet spot." At some point, it will appear to you just how easy that cuts. Strive to maintain that awareness and that sweet spot.

When I was using the 30 degree bowl gouge, I was riding pretty close to the edge. In other words, it was cutting cleanly, but it wouldn't have taken much of a mistake to make a catch. Using the acute bowl gouge, you can see that the position of the tool is totally different. This cut would be much more forgiving than the previous one. Which is best? Probably the acute gouge will be safer from a catch and will still give a decent cut. I use them both; sometimes one will cut a surface better than the other.

The outside diameter of the bowl has been cleaned up and roughly shaped. I am not going to spend a lot of time on it right now as the bowl will later be reversed and the finished form developed then. As you can see, I have put a four jaw chuck onto the lathe. This will hold the base of the bowl by the tenon.

I am using a 3/8" spindle gouge to clean up the surface of the rim.

If you have a small or lightweight lathe and the bowl is really out of round and balance, take a light cleanup cut on the inside of the bowl. This should remove most of the out of balance material and improve vibration, etc., making turning easier. On a heavy lathe this is normally not a problem, but it sure doesn't hurt.

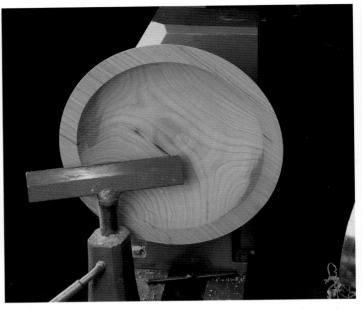

At this point, all I have done is clean up the surface to allow myself enough stock for whatever outside shape I end up with. As you can see, the two sides still have a touch of sealer on them.

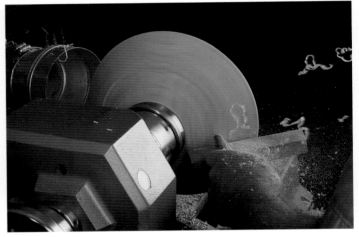

Using the acute bowl gouge, starting to make my form. I am using a normal cut, not a shear cut.

Still shaping.

Sand any imperfections from the back of the bowl.

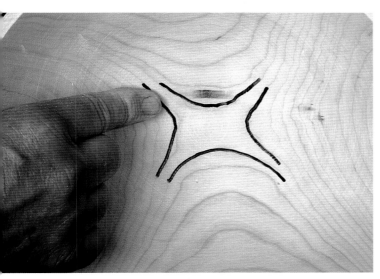

The bottom of the bowl can be a problem area when sanding, especially with this particular grain pattern. The wood inside the lines that I have marked at the very center is called face grain. It sands much easier than end grain (the grain lines). If you sand too much on the bowl, chances are you will sand a hollow onto the face grain. Pay attention as you are sanding and take this into account.

When sanding the top of the rim, I sight down the disc and match the angle of the bowl. There is no reason for me to sand haphazardly and lose all the definition on the rim—after having spent time putting it there. It's the little things that make the whole.

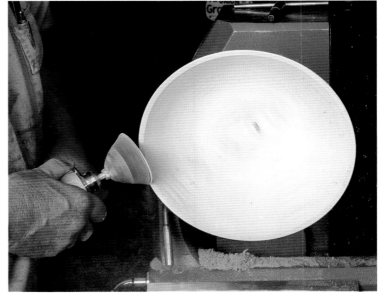

The same holds true with the outside of the rim. Present your disc at the proper angle. I am fortunate in that that this bowl has not gone out of round at all. Of course, on the other hand, I am not done. At times, too aggressive sanding will cause heat, which can put the bowl out of round and cause heat cracks. Sand until you have a good surface, but don't oversand.

I'm sanding now with 180 grit.

I am sure this picture looks like a contradiction as it appears that I am hand sanding with the lathe running. Yes, I am. I'm doing this to burnish the surface, which will make any sanding scratches appear more prominently so I can easily see them.

I have progressed through the grits 120 and 180. Here are a few more tips about power sanding. Occasionally you may have a bad spot, say a bad area of end grain or some little feature that does not clean up. Instead of sanding the entire bowl, stop the lathe and sand that one small area with the lathe off. Then turn the lathe back on and sand again, which will blend that area together with the surrounding areas. Always keep your sanding disc or paper moving—never just sand in one spot. If, as you are working through your grits, you come upon a scratch made by the initial sanding, it is best to go back to a heavier grit and remove that and then continue with your grit progression. If you try to remove the scratch with the finer grit, you will have a tendency to oversand and burnish the surface. I am of the belief that all sanding scratches cannot be removed with the lathe running. At some point, you must hand sand to stop those concentric rings from showing in your work. I normally sand to 180 or 220 grit and then go to silicone carbide paper. I tear my sheets into sixths and fold each sixth into thirds. This gives me a padded sanding paper. It also provides me with three fresh surfaces and many edges to sand up to shoulders, etc., rather than sanding over them and losing my definition.

Doing the same to the rim.

Now the lathe is off and I am hand sanding with the grain as much as possible.

We are ready to start finishing. The very first thing I do is cover the bed of my lathe (or anyone else's that I happen to be working on). It's a pet peeve of mine to take a machine that has treated you well and haphazardly slop it up. Besides, clean tools work better as far as I'm concerned. We will be using Deft™ semigloss straight from the can as a base with tung oil as the finish.

I have finished hand sanding the bowl to 400 grit. I normally do not go higher than this unless it's some exotic type of wood that demands it. The main thing you want is to have all the scratches eliminated. Don't sell sanding short. The finish of your bowl will be a direct reflection of the preparation done for it. The bowl should have that smooth, completed feel before it ever gets a drop of finish.

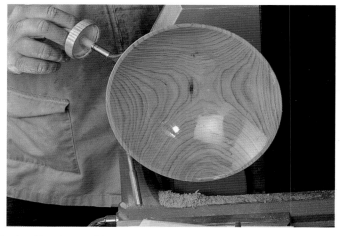

Apply a liberal coat of the Deft™ to the entire bowl. Watch for any thirsty spots and make sure to keep them wet.

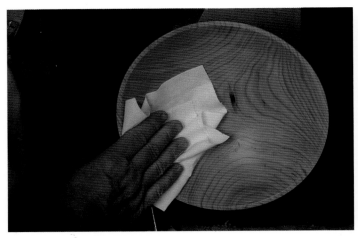

After a couple of minutes, take a paper towel and wipe the excess finish off the bowl with the lathe stopped. I do not use the lathe for any part of the finishing process on the bowl, other than to hold the piece for ease of handling.

Immediately take 0000 steel wool and the oil of your choice and start to scrub the surface. Naturally, the Deft™ is not yet dry so this scrubbing with the oil and steel wool removes it from the surface but leaves it in the pores. The mixture of oil and Deft make a kind of slurry, which again helps fill the pores.

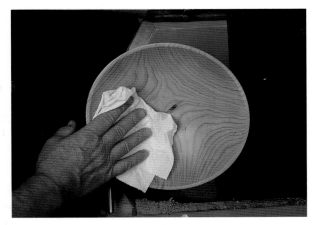

After the finish has soaked in, make sure there are no dry spots (if there are, rewet them), then dry with a paper towel.

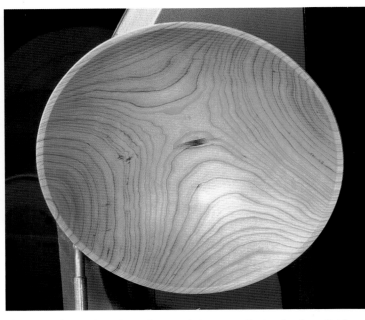

I have wiped everything dry and am ready to reverse the bowl so I can finish the foot.

I will be using a jam chuck to reverse the bowl because it is my favorite method. If a bowl has gone out of round, the force of putting it in the jam chuck will return it to concentric. This action automatically centers the bowl and even allows you to remove it and put it back in without losing any of the concentricity. I know of no other way of doing this that still ensures "repeatability." For example, if you use a four jaw chuck with button jaws (which is meant to hold the bowl on the outside of the rim with rubber buttons) and if the bowl is out of round, chances are it will be slightly off center when being held in the chuck. This is no big problem, as you can blend the foot into the bowl. But if you take the bowl out, putting it back on the same spot is no easy chore. A vacuum chuck holds very well, but your chances of recentering it exactly as you had it the previous time are minimal. Now, you may ask "So what? I'm only going to turn the bottom and don't plan to take it off." Well, have you ever forgotten to check how much material you have left in the bottom of the bowl before putting it on the button jaws or vacuum chuck? I have. I can remove mine and check it instead of inadvertently making a funnel instead of a bowl.

OK, let's get going. Using a faceplate, screw chuck, or a chuck with expanding jaws, mount a piece of scrap for a jam chuck onto the lathe. The scrap block must be larger than the diameter of the bowl, as we will be holding the bowl by its largest diameter at the rim. True up the outside edge of the scrap block and break the edges just to be safe. Then "guesstimate" (or measure if you like) and throw a couple of pencil lines on the jam chuck with the lathe running. This will give us an idea of where to cut our rebate.

Using a parting tool, start to cut a rebate to accept the rim of the bowl. Be sure that the inside of the rim does not contact anything. In other words, make the rebate wide enough that you don't contact any of the inside of the bowl with the jam chuck. The only places you should have contact are between the largest diameter of the bowl's rim and the vertical wall of the jam chuck and the very top of the bowl and the bottom of the rebate. You also want that vertical wall of the jam chuck to be straight. If it is tapered, you may not get a tight solid grip on the bowl. To make the best cut you can, sight down your tool and align it with the bed of the lathe, then push it straight forward.

By matching the bowl to the closest line, I have a visual idea of where to start. The largest pencil line happens to be slightly smaller than the diameter of the bowl, so I know if I stay inside that line I can rough out my first cut without fear of having gone larger than the bowl's diameter.

Testing for fit. We have a little more to go.

Take very light cuts and remember that what you take off one side automatically comes off the other. In other words, if you take off 1/16", in reality you have taken 1/8". Notice the tool alignment to the bed of the lathe.

Starting to remove excess material from the base.

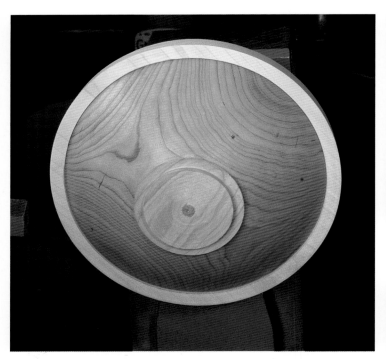

I have reduced the foot slightly and blended the bottom of the bowl to the foot diameter.

When you have reached that right spot, work the bowl into the rebate, as it has to be a tight fit. Once the rim is completely started into the rebate, a good rap with the palm of your hand will normally seat it the rest of the way. Make sure the rim contacts the bottom of the rebate. This helps to prevent any deflection during turning, which will unseat the bowl. Occasionally, you may go too far with the diameter of the rebate. A piece of masking tape around the edge of the bowl or a paper towel between the bowl and the jam chuck (if the bowl is small enough) may remedy this situation. Worse case scenario— you will have to recut the existing rebate deeper but smaller in diameter if the stock allows, or cut a new piece of scrap. Keep in mind that the depth of the rebate need only be slightly deeper than the widest point on the rim—excessive depth will not hold any better.

Just to prove a point, I will take it out and check the bottom.

Using a 3/8" spindle gouge, I am starting to undercut the base.

Using a 1/4" spindle gouge to clean up the base of the foot. At this point, I am going from the center towards the outside for accessibility. In other words, I can ride the bevel of my tool and get a smooth cut.

Still using my 1/4" spindle gouge, I am defining a bead that has kind of become my signature on bowls. It tells people that I have been there and finished off everything neatly, plus I think it looks great.

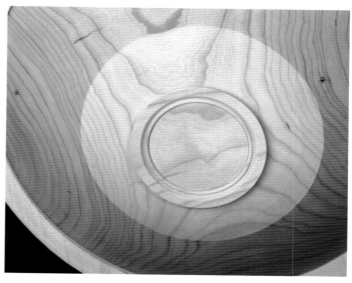

The bead completed.

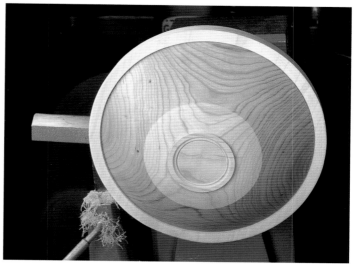

The bottom of the bowl is ready for sanding.

I'm using the Velcro sanding discs to blend the very base of the bowl. Finish sanding the foot and the foot's relief.

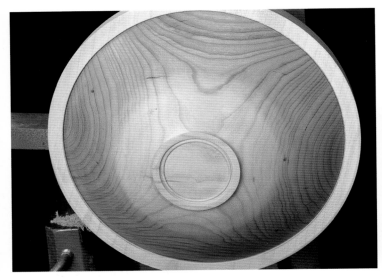

The base is completely sanded and ready to be finished.

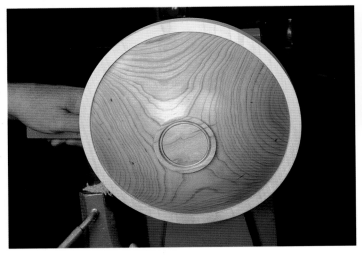

The finished base. I used the same procedure to finish the raw areas as I did to finish the rest of the bowl.

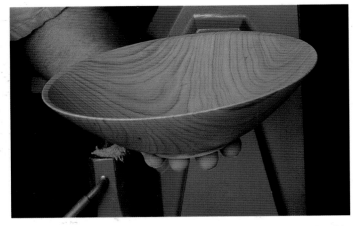

Another view of the finished bowl. Sometimes the fit of the jam chuck will be so tight that it is difficult to remove the bowl, for lack of anywhere to grab it. If this happens, I normally take the jam chuck off the lathe, put my hands underneath the bowl, and rap the jam chuck on something solid, like the ways on the lathe (being careful not to hit the bowl, just the edge of the chuck). This normally does the trick. After I have removed the bowl, I like to give it a complete coat of oil with the 0000 steel wool—inside, outside, the entire bowl. Let it sit for a while (five to ten minutes), then wipe dry.

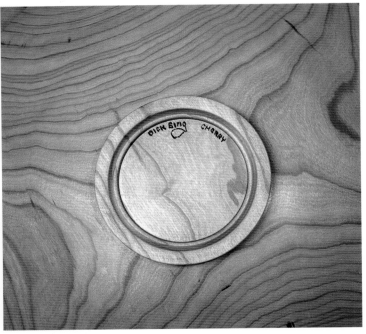

The next day, I normally sign the bowl and identify the species, then give it another coat of oil. The cherry bowl is now done.

Some afterthoughts…The foot on most bowls is normally too large for my liking. I hear other turners tell me that they do this to make the bowl stable. My feeling is that anything put in the bowl runs to the center anyway. I'm sure there are exceptions, but I love the look of a bowl with a small foot and curved bottom; this gives it the illusion of floating above the surface that it is resting on.

Also, if this bowl were to be used for food purposes, I probably would have used mineral oil as a finish and a coat of wax to make it look nicer before use. The finish that I'm using is still safe, however, once the drying agents have evaporated. The care of a bowl used for food involves regularly wiping it out with a warm, damp cloth and drying it. If the surface becomes dry looking, just give it another coat of mineral oil. Remember, I said mineral oil. If you use olive oil, sunflower oil, vegetable oil, or any organic oil, it will turn rancid. Mineral oil will not. Walnut oil is an exception, as it will not turn rancid either. As far as what we can put in a wooden bowl, I think it's basically a matter of common sense. You wouldn't want to put pickled beets in a wooden bowl, for example, unless you wanted to change the color. One of the nicest things about actually using a wooden bowl is the patina that it develops with use; this is something that can be achieved no other way.

The Natural Top Bowl

Sooner or later everyone wants to try a natural top, which is a bowl oriented in the log so that the rim edge contains the bark. Normally these are very delicate looking vessels, used more as decorative objects than as utilitarian bowls. My basic pet peeve on natural tops is when the highs and lows are not balanced. Occasionally I do see some that are unbalanced that still attract me. But these are the oddities, rather than the norm. When I ask fellow turners why their rims are uneven, the usual answer is "I like it like that." I believe if most were really honest, the answer would be "I don't know how to make it any other way." In this section, I will explain the process that I use to balance these highs and lows and create a more uniform bowl.

Looking at the end of this mesquite half log, you can see how I have oriented the layout of the bowl. Laying the diameter of the bowl out on a curved surface with a pair of dividers (or a compass) will give you a blank shaped like a football. An easy way to do this is take a round, appropriately sized object (such as a jam chuck) and position it on the log with a screw. Then band saw this out, using the template as a guide. I also slightly cant my band saw table, which creates a slight cone shape and eliminates part of the base material. This is not necessary, but it's just one of those little things that I like to do.

I am holding a cone dead center and a cone tip live center. The cone dead center (in my left hand) was the forerunner of live centers. These used to be placed in the tailstock, greased or waxed, and they are what held the work in the tailstock before live centers. I use the cone dead center in the headstock to drive the piece. It has some benefits: With the work held between the dead center in the headstock and the live center in the tailstock, it is driven by friction. In other words, we must apply enough pressure on the tailstock to provide friction on the headstock to drive our piece. You must have a live center in the tailstock so there is no drag there. The beauty of this is that if there is a catch, the workpiece just stops. In other words, it slips on the dead center. On a large piece, sometimes using this method means you cannot work the piece as fast as you could with other methods, but I will put up with the inconvenience for all the advantages. If I used a four prong drive, chances are I would not be resting on all four prongs with the configuration of the surface. This would allow the piece to come out of the lathe at times, for lack of holding ability. A two prong drive would probably be a better choice than the four.

Here is the bowl blank separated from the log after being band sawn. It is ready to be roughed out.

Go ahead and put the workpiece into the lathe. The headstock can be centered to the screw hole we used on the template; just set the tailstock end by eye. Bring up your tool rest until you are relatively close to your piece.

On a natural edge bowl, you have two sets of heights or, as I call them, points. When cutting out the blank, the two points on the top will be the high points. When the blank is sawn out, two additional points are developed: the low points. These sets of points are not always equal in height as they are dependent on the contours of the log. These four points are what we are going to balance to make the highs equal in height and the lows equal in height. This will give a balanced rim to the bowl's shape. Place your finger on the tool rest in line with one of the low points. This will be a quick reference; hold this position.

With the hand wheel, roll over to the other side of the piece and compare the two surfaces for uniformity. Not bad.

Now we will move to the high side of the bark, or high points. Again, place your finger at one of the high sides as a reference.

Again, roll the work piece to the opposite side and check the position of that bark. As you can see, it is considerably lower than the opposite side.

We are going to change the tailstock location to balance this out. We only want to change our high points, not the low points (which are uniform), so we must make sure we don't change the height of the piece at the tailstock, which would alter the lows. To make this adjustment, the high points should be horizontal to the lathe (your eyesight will be plenty accurate). In my case, I have to loosen the tailstock and shift the tailstock end of the blank towards the tool rest without changing the plane that it is already on. My move was about 1/2" towards the tool rest.

Lightly retighten the tailstock. Changing the bottom of the blank towards the tool rest raises the low point and lowers the high point. As you did before, place your finger at one high point, then compare to the other. Repeat this process until the two high points agree. My low points happened to agree, but if they had not I would have done the same to them as we did with the high point—in other words, shifting the point on the tailstock whichever way is necessary to make them agree in height. In extreme cases, you may want to shift the headstock point as well. By the way, this type of setup between centers is not reserved just for natural top bowls. If you have a normal shaped bowl and can't get at something or want to alter your position to get away from a knot or other imperfection (or even want to include one), this same process can be used.

Before you turn the lathe on, remember that because of the adjustment we have made, our relatively balanced piece of wood has been repositioned to one that is now lopsided and out of balance. When I took the bark off my piece, it gave a better surface for the dead center in the headstock to drive. You may want to check yours to see if the cone center is filled with bark. If it is, clean it out. Turn your speed down. Make sure the tailstock is locked down tightly and enough pressure is applied. My piece, as you can see by the shadow on the far side, is out of balance, especially on the tailstock end. This one is not too severe. At times, it can be very severe, however, so set your lathe speed accordingly. Before you touch that button, position your tool rest and hand roll the workpiece to make sure there is no interference.

Checking the bark, I noticed that better than half of it was loose. I could have tried to glue it down, but it had been loose for some time and evidently warped, so once glued the bark and bowl would no longer match each other. Therefore, I just pulled it off. The remainder of the bark is adhered quite solidly. At this point, I will not pry or scrape it off as I may damage the rim and I do not know yet where my form is going to end up. Regarding the look of bark on a bowl, I personally don't like big heavy scaly bark on a delicate bowl. I do leave bark on, but normally it is when I'm using wood from trees with a smooth bark, like apple or pear. Bark from walnut and oak does nothing for me. If you do intend to keep the bark on, always check to make sure that is secure. Normally at this stage, there is no problem. If there are spots where the bark is loose, you can usually take some thin cyanoacrylate and glue them down. Keep checking the bark as you develop your form. Before you make your final cut, take the thin cyanoacrylate and apply between the bowl and the bottom of the bark, trying not to get any on the top bark surface—otherwise it will not look natural. Be very careful if you use accelerator, as it can create a white residue that may be impossible to clean off the bark, which again will not look natural. If necessary, the same procedure can be used on the inside of the bowl. A natural top bowl with no bark and an undisturbed surface where the bark would have been, is one of my favorites—the area where the bark was attached shows all kinds of interesting bumps and growing textures. To me, this can be more interesting if it's done well. Another feature normally found on natural top bowls is a band of sapwood that circles the rim. This is another nice contrasting element.

Start truing up your blank. As it gets more concentric, take a cut towards the low points and make sure you leave a ridge, or witness mark. Do the same with the high points. Stop the lathe and check the relationship of the points to each other. Sometimes, as you reduce the diameter of your block, the shape of the top may change the points. As it is right now, mine are about 1/16" from being uniform, which for roughing out a piece to be dried is quite adequate.

I am starting to develop a form on the bowl. When you get out past the low points, you will start windmilling (in other words, half the bowl has no stock). Make sure you don't press too hard—you want to continue cutting in the plane that you were going and kind of float your tool over those low spots and maintain contact with the high spots. This is another place where body movement is your salvation. Strictly using arm movements will produce jerky motions. Lock your arms to your body and make your body move the tool.

I am using a 3/8" spindle gouge to cut a tenon for a chuck. Be sure to face off the very bottom of the tenon so that it can seat against the jaws of the chuck.

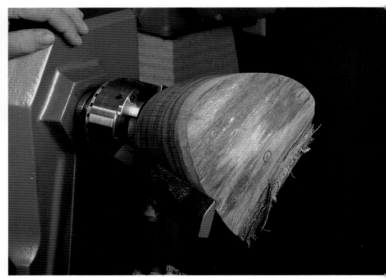

I have put the blank into a chuck and it is being held by the tenon.

One of the hardest parts to turn on a bowl is the very center. As we go towards the center our cutting speed slows down. I "guesstimate" how deep I want to hollow out my piece by taking my 3/8" spindle gouge and placing it alongside the bowl. Marking the depth of the hole that I want with my thumb positioned on the tool, I place the tip at the exact center—where the tool becomes very much like a drill. Line up your tool with the ways of the lathe, keeping it parallel to the bed of the lathe, and push forward. Clean the chips out often. When the depth is at your thumb in relation to the top of the bowl, you are done. Now we can hollow out the bowl without that slow, slow spot in the middle and when we reach the bottom of the hole we should be at the depth we want. If you have any bark left on, keep in mind that you will be reducing its holding ability as you work the bowl. Be careful that it doesn't fly off. If it is already loose, go ahead and remove it.

When I am cleaning the bowl out, I like my 30 degree gouge to do the edges of the wings. The other one will work, this one just seems to work better for me. Once I get past the wings, I will switch to the other gouge.

Continuing to hollow out the inside of the bowl. Remember to watch your fingers on those flying wings.

The bowl is now roughed out. Date it, identify the species, and give it a coat of green wood sealer (or dry using the process of your choice). I chose to dry this bowl because, as I said before, I like my finished turnings round. A lot of people like a little extra distortion in a natural top and therefore complete the bowl while still green (or wet). If you decide to turn and finish the bowl green, it has to be turned quite thin to give it more freedom to move without cracking. Also by turning it thin, you will reduce the moisture content. Some of the moisture will be thrown out due to centrifugal forces and, as you sand, the heat will reduce the moisture even more. During sanding, you must be careful that you don't create heat cracks from getting the surface too warm. In addition, the bowl must be completed in one operation from start to

finish, or it will warp out of round. By this I mean don't start in the morning, break for coffee, and decide to finish it up tomorrow. It will warp up so bad that you will have a difficult time handling it, if it is even still possible. Given the possibility of Aunt Rose stopping by after you have started but are not too far along, you *could* take a plastic bag, put some of the wet shavings in it, and put it over the bowl on your lathe. This will stop most of the air flow around the bowl and hopefully stop some of the drying that causes distortion as well.

Here is a piece of hard maple that has been roughed out and dried. Naturally it has distorted while drying. I am going to use the chuck instead of a scrap block to drive it and hold the bottom with my live center. This is just convenient.

I have placed the bowl over the chuck, which contacts the inside, but not in a holding mode. I brought up the tailstock and located the live center on the witness mark left during rough turning, then tightened the tailstock down. If your chuck does not fit the bowl due to the bowl's contours or for some other reason, put a piece of scrap on a faceplate that does come closer to its diameter. This will replace the chuck.

The first step is to lightly clean up the areas close to the highs and lows. I used a 3/8" spindle gouge for this. If you have to balance the piece, use the same technique as we did during the green turning. Check the lows…

I have placed the bowl's tenon into the jaws of the chuck and tightened it securely.

…and the highs. When both are balanced to your satisfaction, clean up the tenon and start cleaning up the remaining form.

Using a 3/8" spindle gouge, use a drawing cut from the bottom. This is not a shear cut, as the bevel is rubbing. The reason I am doing this is that I cannot get in the correct position to take a normal cut.

Rough in your form (it does not have to be perfect at this point). Half of the bark was missing from this bowl. It seemed secure but a couple of raps with the butt of the tool handle removed the remainder. If this had not worked, I would have waited till closer to the end after hollowing out so there would have been much less surface for the bark to adhere to.

Now I have enough clearance to take a cut in the normal mode to the end of the rim.

I'm happy with my form at this point. Next I am using my 9/16" spindle gouge to very lightly shear cut the surface. Any form of shear scraping with any tool will work here; I am using the 9/16" gouge because of the long handle that lays against my thigh, giving me a little more control on the ends of the wings. Again, your movements need to be smooth, so use your body to move your cutting tool.

I was getting some slight undulations or marks in the high wings. It is a must that this area be clean and smooth, as the majority will have to be hand sanded to keep a crisp edge on the edge of the rim. I switched to my shear scraper hoping I could make smoother movements. If you'll notice, both hands are holding the blade and the handle is under my forearm. This allows me to move more fluidly and uniformly with the tool.

The most critical part of turning the inside is starting the cut on the tips of the wings, which are windmilling. I like to use my 3/8" spindle gouge, as I can see and control it better than a bowl gouge. When you start your cut, take it lightly. Don't be a bear about it, practice on it. Take light cuts and get a sense of how your body moves to make a fluid, uniform cut.

I am cutting a little deeper than the low points. I want to keep as much strength in that bowl as I can for stability reasons but I also want to be past the rim when I go to finish the remainder of the bowl. It would be very difficult to try and pick up a cut on the wings. I am not going to hollow out the interior with the 3/8" spindle gouge; I will be switching to the bowl gouge.

When you have practiced that entering cut and reached the thickness of the wall that you intend to have, take a final, very light cut—as smooth and uniform as you can. If you'll notice, my left hand is cupped around the outside of the bowl to help dampen any vibration. This is a very gentle smooth cut, reminiscent of a naked person crawling through a barbed wire fence. Once I've made that final cut, if there are still any imperfections I take my 3/8" spindle gouge and do a very, very light shear scrape from the inside out. Again, this is a very fluid gentle cut. If you become brutish, chances are it will vibrate and catch. And if your wings are as thin as most people want them, chances are you will break a wing. Yes, this will be sanded later, but I prefer to have it as clean as I can to keep the rim as sharp and crisp as possible.

What you are striving for is a nice clean wall with a uniform clean surface all the way to the rim.

I have switched to my acute angle bowl gouge and am taking material out of the center.

Using care, I am picking up another cut, as discussed previously with another bowl (see page 35). With the thinness of this bowl, picking up the cut becomes even more critical to avoid ridges. Being thin, this bowl will have a tendency to go out of round, especially when sanding (even though it is dry), and sanding out those ridges will be even more difficult.

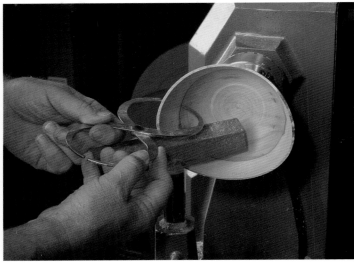

Using the double end calipers, check your wall thickness for uniformity. Mine right now is approximately 1/8". It's still a little heavy in the bottom.

Making the bottom uniform.

I have cleaned out the bowl to the depth and wall thickness that I feel is sufficient. With a heavy radiused scraper, I am truing up the very bottom. I am not taking a lot of wood, I am just enhancing the surface.

While cleaning out the bottom, I could feel a "pick up ridge" on the side. The shape of the scraper was a perfect match to the bowl's contour, but it would have covered too large of an area and I know full well it would have vibrated and probably caught. In other words, I would have presented too large of a cutting surface and overstressed it. So I stood the scraper up in a shear cut mode and eliminated it in that manner.

We are ready to sand.

This bowl is a prime example of what I was referring to when I talked about picking up the cut and leaving little ridges that would be difficult to remove if the bowl went out of round. I have one little spot in the wing that did not come out conventionally with the shear scraping, as I didn't want to go too thin with the wall thickness. Therefore, I have put a 100 grit disc on a Velcro holder and—with the lathe stopped and the bowl cradled in my hand below the imperfection—I use the drill to power sand that area, keeping the disc as flat as I can and not coming into contact with the rim. In so many words, I spot sanded the imperfection out.

I don't want to use the 100 grit on the whole bowl as it does not warrant it. I have put on a 120 grit disc and gone over the area I spot sanded with the lathe stopped. Now I have turned on the lathe and am sanding the bowl. Work inside and outside, being careful around the rim. If you sand the rim with the lathe running, the edge coming to you will get rounded, which we do not want. Power sand below the rim; we will basically hand sand the rest. If you have a bad area on the outside of the wing, power sand it with the lathe stopped, as before. This is why I like a variable speed drill motor—I can slow the speed down and handle the drill in delicate areas. The rest of the outside (minus the rim) can also be power sanded.

Sanding the outside of the bowl.

Hand sanding at the rim area.

The bowl is ready for finishing.

Apply a liberal coat of Deft™ to the entire bowl. Watch for any dry spots and keep them wet.

Scrub oil over the Deft™ with 0000 steel wool.

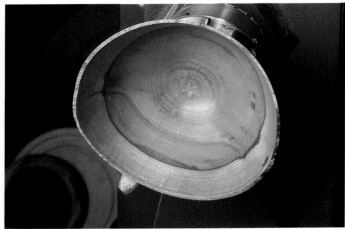

The bowl has been wiped dry and is ready to be reversed. Sometimes when the finish gets in the bark, it becomes difficult to remove any excess, which will, if allowed to dry, become very shiny in comparison to the rest of the bark. I find a toothbrush very handy to scrub out that excess oil. In fact, I find a toothbrush very handy to get oil and finish out of many nooks and crannies, not just on bowls with bark.

I have put a screw chuck on the spindle and a piece of MDF that was from an old jam chuck. I radiused the edges and covered them with a foam type tape. The reason I did this was to help protect the inside of the bowl and provide a little more positive driving surface.

Using a 3/8" spindle gouge to start forming my rim.

Making a smooth cut for our wall thickness, still with the bowl gouge. My left hand is dampening the vibration of the bowl.

Using a bowl gouge to start removing the material from inside the bowl. As you remove the insides, remember how this bowl is attached. We are on a small dovetail with not a lot of wood remaining around it. The wood is brittle and does not cut very well, so I am taking a good cut without being overly aggressive.

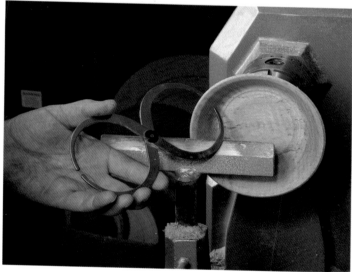

Checking wall thickness with the double end calipers. Right now it is slightly over 3/16".

Removing more material with the bowl gouge.

Refining the inside shape to match the outside.

I have thinned the wall thickness so it is now uniform.

I am sanding with the Velcro disc. Due to the coarseness of the wood, I am starting with 100 grit.

Using the heavy radiused scraper to refine the bottom of the bowl.

Progress through your grits and hand sanding, as previously described.

Ready to sand.

Apply finish to complete the inside of the bowl.

I have taken our finished bowl off the chuck.

If I had been in a production mode and felt I could get away with the base as it is (with the dovetail), I would have sanded and finished it before I put it on the chuck. However, I do not like an exposed dovetail that says "this is how I held the bowl." After looking at the bowl from a distance, I also felt that the foot could be slightly smaller, which will give the bowl the appearance of more lift when it is sitting on a flat surface. However, because of the recess, I am limited in terms of how much I can adjust this…so I will make do. I am still going to eliminate the dovetail by jam chucking. Another means of reversing the bowl would be to use a vacuum chuck to hold it.

I have put on a piece of MDF and am cutting a rebate with my parting tool.

The bowl is mounted in the jam chuck and I am ready to finish the recess on the foot.

Using a 1/4" spindle gouge, I am turning the dovetail into my signature bead. I am still unhappy with the diameter of the foot, so I am going to decrease it.

Reducing the diameter of the foot. Because of this reduction, I will also need to blend in the very bottom of the bowl.

Blending the bowl into the smaller diameter foot.

Ready for sanding.

Looking straight on, you can see that the bowl has a steady, continuous curve to the foot. If you would carry that curve through the foot, it would almost be ball-like.

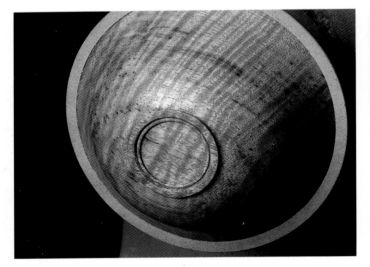

The base has been sanded and finished, using the same process as before. To me, the dovetailed recess now reflects a finished bowl, since it has a bead and no visible means of how it was held. Creating the smaller diameter foot and having to blend in the base of the bowl to it is a step that most people probably would not do. If my sole living came from the speed of turning bowls, I may have let it go as well, depending on how hungry I was at the time. But, given my personal makeup, I still might have changed it to satisfy me. If you are going to create something, create it as a reflection of you—put your heart and soul into it. "Just OK" is not enough…after all, we are not digging ditches.

When viewed from an angle, such as walking by a table, the bowl gives an illusion of floating above the surface it is resting on. To me, that's one of the things bowls are all about. Getting there is well worth the extra effort.

How I Sign My Work

People often look at my signature on my turnings and ask how I do it. Number one, I happen to be blessed with a legible writing. This makes it easier. I use a wood burning pen and will be happy to walk you through the procedure that I use. There are various techniques learned through experience over the years. Pay attention as this is hot off the pen.

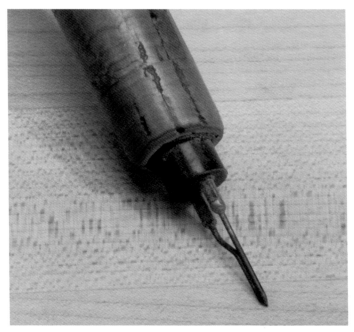

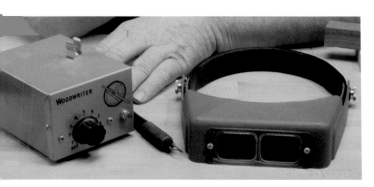

The equipment that I use is simply a woodburning unit with a rheostat that will allow variable temperature settings. The pen itself is a signature tip which has been modified. And, even if you have good vision, some type of magnification is needed.

And here is a top view. To start with, I took a smooth, 6" mill file and worked the point close to what it is now. I made it much more pointed, with less material, than its standard design. When I got close to my desired shape, I took a fine stone and refined the point even more, until it reached its present state. The point should be smooth, with no facets, so it sort of glides on the writing surface. As you can see, there isn't a lot of material holding the top and bottom wires together. If you turned the heat up as high as it would go, I'm sure it would melt the tip. Oops. . . Instead, I treat the tip as fragile, using a lower heat and working my way up, rather than starting too hot and working my way down. Using it this way has not given me any problems, and this particular tip is at least twelve years old. I do have a backup. If I didn't, I'm sure I would have burned out the original one years ago – Murphy's Law again. If you modify your tip as such and use it with care, yours should last a reasonable length of time as well.

Here is a side view of the pen's tip.

I always told myself my vision was good, and it is. But when trying to sign my name and some information on wood, I realized, as I improved, that I had to see – really see – what I was doing. To do this I use a magnifying visor. Any kind of magnification, such as a magnifying light or anything else you do not have to hold in your hand, would be adequate.

Wood itself is the largest variable in writing on wood. The finer the grain and the harder the texture, the better the writing. A piece of hard maple with its uniform grain and hard texture allows you to write on it beautifully. On the other hand, a piece of white oak with its coarse grain, large pores, and distinction between winter growth and summer growth presents problems. Looking down on the growth rings on a tree, you can see each year's growth—under close scrutiny, you can distinguish the winter growth from the summer growth. The summer growth comprises the majority of the annual ring because of its growth through the end of spring, summer, and the beginning of fall. Because this larger area was produced relatively fast, it is softer than the winter growth. During the winter, when the tree becomes dormant and the sap retreats, the tree is still growing. Under the adverse conditions of winter the growth is very minute and much harder.

As you can see, this disc of hard maple accepts writing very easily.

Walnut can be good or can be bad, depending on the coarseness of the grain. On this piece, the writing labeled (1) is totally different than the writing labeled (2). Number 2 had the heat turned up too high and I was pressing too hard.

Here are a few illustrations on oak. The first one, labeled (1), is how I would normally sign oak. I find it quite legible. The second, labeled (2), has the heat turned up, probably a little too high. The third, labeled (3), has the heat turned down but I was pressing against the wood too hard. What does this mean? The real secret to writing on wood is not to burn into the wood, but to write *on* the surface. This is where the magnification enters into the picture. You have to be able to see that you are gently writing on the wood, and that the heat—not the pressure—is burning the wood. When you press too hard, the pen follows the variation between the winter growth and the summer growth and creates a situation just as if it were going down a washboard. This results in very little darkness on the winter growth and a deep black area on the summer growth – or very non uniform writing. Additionally, my signature and information is written very small. Not because I am ashamed of my work, but because I would rather not take away from it. Here again, the fine tip and being able to see with the magnification is a definite help.

Before signing one of your treasures, take a piece of scrap, preferably the same wood as your project, and practice. Don't practice on a fresh saw cut, use a scrap that has been surfaced so that it replicates the actual surface of your project. Normally, you sign your work after your project has had finish applied to it. The finish will burn or flash up around the burned area. When you have completed the signing, therefore, take some 0000 steel wool and lightly scrub the surface of the burned area. This will clean up those flashings and leave much more legible writing. Then hit it with a little of your finish. I'm sure I have missed something and will probably think of it after this book has been published. But as of now, this is Dick Sing—signing off.

Gallery

Natural top maple. 5" x 7-1/2" dia.

Redbud. 2" x 5-1/2" dia.

Bird's eye maple. 2-3/4" x 7" dia.

Hard maple. 3-1/2" x 6-1/2" dia.

Cherry. 2-1/2" x 6-1/2" dia.

Pistachio. 3" x 7-1/4" dia.

Plum. 3-3/4" x 8-1/2" dia.

Hawthorn. 5" x 8-1/2" dia.

Natural top cherry. 3-3/4" x 5-1/2" dia.

Ambrosia maple. 2" x 11" dia.

Bird's eye maple. 2-1/2" x 12-1/2" dia.

Walnut. 5-1/4" x 13-3/4" dia.

Hard maple. 4-1/2" x 13-3/4" dia.

Walnut. 2-1/4" x 6-1/2" dia.

Cherry (project made in book). 3" x 10-1/2" dia.

Walnut (project made in book). 2-1/2" x 6-1/2" dia.

Cherry and walnut bowls together.

Both natural top bowls.

Hawthorn, hard maple, bird's eye maple.

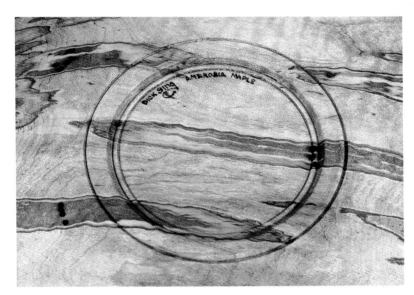

Ambrosia maple bottom, with signature.

Plum, pistachio, cherry.

Bird's eye maple bottom, with signature.

Hawthorn bottom, with signature.